NATURE GUIDE TO
ACADIA
NATIONAL PARK

Help Us Keep This Guide Up to Date

Every effort has been made by the authors and editors to make this guide as accurate and useful as possible. However, many things can change after a guide is published—regulations change, facilities come under new management, and so forth.

We would love to hear from you concerning your experiences with this guide and how you feel it could be improved and kept up to date. While we may not be able to respond to all comments and suggestions, we'll take them to heart, and we'll also make certain to share them with the authors. Please send your comments and suggestions to falconeditorial@globepequot.com.

Thanks for your input!

NATURE GUIDE TO
ACADIA
NATIONAL PARK

ANN SIMPSON AND ROB SIMPSON

FALCONGUIDES

Essex, Connecticut

FALCONGUIDES®

An imprint of The Globe Pequot Publishing Group, Inc.
64 South Main Street
Essex, CT 06426
www.GlobePequot.com

Falcon and FalconGuides are registered trademarks and Make Adventure Your Story is a trademark of The Rowman & Littlefield Publishing Group, Inc.

Distributed by NATIONAL BOOK NETWORK

British Library Cataloguing in Publication Information available

Library of Congress Cataloging-in-Publication Data available

ISBN 978-1-4930-7453-2 (paper: alk. paper)
ISBN 978-1-4930-7454-9 (electronic)

Printed in India

CONTENTS

CONTENTS

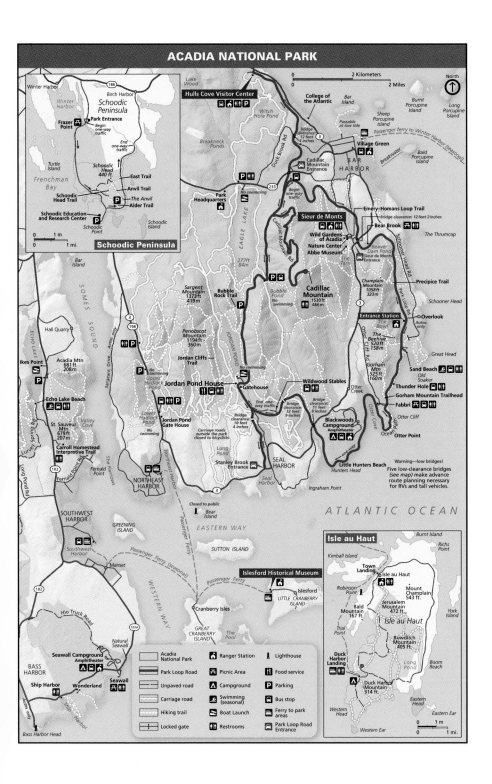

ACADIA NATIONAL PARK

North

0   2 Kilometers
0   2 Miles

Schoodic Peninsula

Winter Harbor
186
Birch Harbor
Winter Harbor
Schoodic Peninsula
Frazer Point
Park Entrance
Begin one-way traffic
End one-way traffic
Turtle Island
Schoodic Head 440 ft.
East Trail
Frenchman Bay
Anvil Trail
Schoodic Head Trail
The Anvil
Alder Trail
Schoodic Education and Research Center
Schoodic Point
Schoodic Island
Bar Island

0   1 m
0   1 mi.

Lake Wood
Hulls Cove Visitor Center
Witch Hole Pond
Breakneck Ponds
Duck Brook Rd
Bridge clearance: 12 feet 4 inches
3
Park Headquarters
233
Begin one-way traffic
No swimming
EAGLE LAKE
277ft 84m
SOMES SOUND
Hall Quarry
3
198
Sargent Mountain 1373ft 419m
Bubble Rock Trail
Bubble Pond No swimming
Penobscot Mountain 1194ft 360m
JORDAN POND
Jordan Cliffs Trail
No swimming
Ikes Point
Acadia Mtn 681 ft 208m
Upper Hadlock Pond
Jordan Pond House
Gatehouse
Echo Lake Beach
St. Sauveur Mtn 679ft 207m
Lower Hadlock Pond
Jordan Pond Gate House
No swimming
Carroll Homestead Interpretive Trail
102
Fernald Point
The Narrows
NORTHEAST HARBOR
Bridge clearance: 10 feet 4 inches
Carriage roads outside the park closed to bicyclists
Long Pond
Stanley Brook Entrance
End one-way traffic
Bridge clearance: 10 feet 9 inches
SEAL HARBOR
3
Seal Harbor
SOUTHWEST HARBOR
GREENING ISLAND
Closed to public
Bear Island
EASTERN WAY
Southwest Harbor
Passenger Ferry (seasonal)
SUTTON ISLAND
Manset
102
WESTERN WAY
Hio Truck Road
102A
Natural Seawall
Seawall Campground Amphitheater
BASS HARBOR
Ship Harbor
Wonderland
Seawall
Passenger Ferry
GREAT CRANBERRY ISLAND
The Pool
Islesford Historical Museum
Islesford
LITTLE CRANBERRY ISLAND
Cranberry Isles
Bass Harbor Head

College of the Atlantic
Bar Island
Burnt Porcupine Island
Long Porcupine Island
Sheep Porcupine Island
Passable at low tide
Passenger ferry to Winter Harbor (seasonal)
Village Green
Bald Porcupine Island
Breakwater
Cadillac Mountain Entrance
BAR HARBOR
Sieur de Monts
Wild Gardens of Acadia
Nature Center
Abbe Museum
Beaver Dam Pond
The Tarn
Sieur de Monts Entrance
Emery-Homans Loop Trail
Bridge clearance: 12 feet 2 inches
Bear Brook
The Thrumcap
Champlain Mountain 1058ft 323m
Precipice Trail
Cadillac Mountain 1530ft 466m
Schooner Head
Entrance Station
Overlook
Autos only
Cadillac Mountain Rd
The Bowl
The Beehive 520ft 158m
Great Head
Gorham Mtn 525ft 160m
Sand Beach
Old Soaker
Thunder Hole
Wildwood Stables
Otter Creek
Gorham Mountain Trailhead
Fabbri
Otter Cliff
Blackwoods Campground Amphitheater
Otter Point
Ocean
Otter Cove
Little Hunters Beach
Hunters Head
Ingraham Point

Warning—low bridges!
Five low-clearance bridges (see map) make advance route planning necessary for RVs and tall vehicles.

Bridge clearance: 11 feet 8 inches
Bridge clearance: 11 feet 9 inches

Park Loop Rd
Otter Cliff Rd
Schooner Head Rd
Park Loop Rd

ATLANTIC OCEAN

Isle au Haut

Burnt Island
Richs Point
Kimball Island
Town Landing
Isle au Haut
Robinson Point
Mount Champlain 543 ft.
Jerusalem Mountain 472 ft.
York Island
Bald Mountain 167 ft.
Trial Point
Isle au Haut
Bowditch Mountain 405 ft.
Duck Harbor Landing
Long Pond
Boom Beach
Duck Harbor Mountain 314 ft.
Western Head
Eastern Head
Western Ear
Eastern Ear

0   1 m
0   1 mi.

Legend

Acadia National Park		Ranger Station		Lighthouse
Park Loop Road		Picnic Area		Food service
Unpaved road		Campground		Parking
Carriage road		Swimming (seasonal)		Bus stop
Hiking trail		Boat Launch		Ferry to park areas
Locked gate		Restrooms		Park Loop Road Entrance

ACADIA NATIONAL PARK: THE BASICS

History and Facts

Established: July 8, 1916, Sieur de Monts National Monument; February 26, 1916, Lafayette National Park; January 19, 1929, Acadia National Park

Visitors: 3,970,260

Designations: Sites on the National Register of Historic Places include Baker Island Light Station, Bass Harbor Head Light Station, Bear Island Light Station, Carriage Paths Bridges and Gatehouses, Islesford Historical Museum

Natural Historic Places: Schoodic Peninsula Historic District, Blackwoods and Seawall Campgrounds, Historic carriage roads and gatehouses

National Register of Historic Places: Island-wide trail system, 18 memorial plaques, 12 viewpoints

State: Maine

Counties: Hancock and Knox

Time zone: Eastern Standard Time (EST)

Official park website: www.nps.gov/acad

Physical Features

Acreage: 47,748, including 12,416 acres privately owned under conservation easement and managed by the National Park Service

Elevation: Lowest point: 0' at sea level; highest point: 1,530' at Cadillac Mountain summit

Significant mountains: 26

Water resources: 110 lakes and ponds, 24+ streams, 60 miles of Atlantic Ocean coastline, 1,179 acres of nontidal marshy lands

Wetlands: 4,000+ acres

Average annual precipitation: 55.54"

Average annual snowfall: 66.1"

Temperature range (F): -21°F to 96°F; mean annual temperature 47.3°F

Plant species: 1,100+ species of vascular plants including approximately 200 species of trees and shrubs, 650 herbaceous species including wildflowers, 200 grasses and sedges, 50 ferns and fern allies; 400+ lichens; 400+ fungi; 300+ nonvascular plants including mosses, liverworts, and hornworts, 80+ species of freshwater aquatic plants

Animal species: About 338 birds, 45 mammals, 31 fish, 7 reptiles, 11 amphibians, 53 butterflies

Wildlife population estimates: 1,600 harbor seals; 40 gray seals

Facilities

Entrance stations: 1—Park Loop Road 1 mile north of Sand Beach

Visitor center: Hulls Cove Visitor Center

Contact stations: Sieur de Monts Nature Center, Rockefeller Hall, Islesford Museum

Roads: 21 miles of gravel road, 68 miles of paved road, including 27 miles of Park Loop Road

Trails: 145 miles of hiking trails

Carriage roads: 45 miles

Campgrounds: 4—2 on Mount Desert Island: Blackwoods (281 sites), Seawall (202 sites); Schoodic Peninsula: Schoodic Woods (89 sites); Isle au Haut Duck Harbor (5 sites)

Picnic areas: 6—5 on Mount Desert Island: Bear Brook (35 sites), Seawall (14 sites), Pretty Marsh (11 sites), Thompson Island (46 sites), Fabbri (23 sites); Schoodic Peninsula: Frazer Point (26 sites)

Lodging: No lodging in the park but many options in the surrounding area

Dining: 1—Jordan Pond House Restaurant

ACKNOWLEDGMENTS

Many thanks to the superb park personnel and volunteers of Acadia National Park who have dedicated their lives to preserving the natural resources of the park and sharing the natural wonders of the park with visitors. We would particularly like to thank the staff at Schoodic Institute, especially Seth Benz, Nick Fisichelli, and Sarah Luchini. Michael Marion and Oliver Cygan added their knowledge and expertise of peregrines and other natural resources in the park. We are appreciative of Becky Marvil and all the staff and volunteers

Park rangers share their knowledge of nature with visitors during informative ranger programs.

ACKNOWLEDGMENTS

that make the Acadia Birding Festival possible. We thank all the staff at the Mount Desert Island Oceanarium, especially Ben Segee. A special thanks to the gurus of Maine birding, Bob Duchesne and Derek Lovitch, for all their help and insight into helping us find and photograph some spectacular birds of Maine. Our thanks also go to the Friends of Acadia for their continued support of the park. We would also like to thank all the staff at Rowman & Littlefield, especially David Legere, whose support and efforts have continued to make this National Park Nature Guide series a reality.

We would like to dedicate this book to our family, including our children and their spouses, Jeremiah, Mitzi, Jessie, Aaron, and especially James, who helped process the pictures for the book and provided the mink image. Also, our grandchildren Georgia, Gracie, Jacob, and Natalie, who remind us that a moment spent sharing nature with a child is an investment in the future of our world. Our heartfelt remembrance goes out to the family of Captain Andy Patterson, whose love of showing visitors the wonders of puffins and other birds on the Bold Coast made a lifelong impact on the lives of many people.

To the reader, we hope this guide helps you enjoy the amazing wonders of nature and, in doing so, generates a spark of love for the plants and animals that rely on us for their continued existence in important natural habitats such as those in Acadia National Park.

PARTNERS WITH ACADIA

Friends of Acadia

Friends of Acadia is Acadia National Park's "Friends Group." Friends groups are philanthropic partners who can fundraise on behalf of the park. Friends of

Acadia preserves, protects, and promotes stewardship of the outstanding natural beauty, ecological vitality, and distinctive cultural resources of Acadia National Park and surrounding communities for the inspiration and enjoyment of current and future generations.

Friends of Acadia is a private, nonprofit organization dedicated to ensuring the long-term protection of the natural and cultural resources of Acadia National Park and its region. To meet this mission, Friends of Acadia channels private donations to conservation and historic preservation projects in the park, monitors planning and legislative activities affecting Acadia, and sponsors volunteer groups in Acadia and surrounding communities. For more information about Friends of Acadia or to join, call (207) 288-3340 or (800) 625-0321 or visit friendsofacadia.org.

Schoodic Institute

Schoodic Institute is Acadia National Park's primary partner in science and education. Partnering with Acadia's science experts, they manage the largest of eighteen National Park Service Research Learning

The Schoodic Institute supports scientific research and education for visitors.

Centers in the United States and are national leaders in the development of new techniques to involve the public in science and conservation. Education is integrated with research programs through public programs and events; they also provide professional development for teachers. For more information, call (207) 288-1310 or visit schoodicinstitute.org.

America's National Park Stores

America's National Parks Stores operates the park store, and proceeds from the store support interpretation and education projects. The store provides high-quality educational products and services to visitors to America's national parks and other public trusts; the association's contributions have benefited parks and visitors by supporting research, educational, and interpretive projects and by funding publications. Just by shopping at the park store you can support your park! Call (207) 288-4988 or visit shop.americasnationalparks .org/store/home/4024/Acadia-National-Park.

Island Explorer Bus Service

Downeast Transportation provides bus service to Acadia National Park visitors fare-free thanks to support from the Friends of Acadia, L.L.Bean, and park entrance fees. The Island Explorer travels throughout Acadia National Park, Mount Desert Island towns, and Schoodic Peninsula. See their website for current maps and timetables. Call (207) 667-5796 or visit downeasttrans.org.

The fare-free Island Explorer buses link destinations on Mount Desert Island with those in the park.

INTRODUCTION

The *Nature Guide to Acadia National Park* is an easy-to-use field guide to help visitors identify some of the most common plants, animals, and natural features of the park. Technical terms have been kept to a minimum, and color pictures accompany the descriptions. This field guide is filled with interesting information about each organism, including natural history and ethnobotanical notes and other historical remarks. We care about the things we know. Intended as an introduction to nature in Acadia National Park, this book will hopefully spark an interest in the natural world and generate further interest in caring for and supporting the environment. You can check the "References" section at the end of this book for more information and resources for in-depth identification purposes.

About Acadia National Park

Surrounded by the cool waters of the Gulf of Maine, Acadia National Park boasts natural beauty with rocky shores, massive granite domes, verdant marshes, and evergreen forests. More than picture-perfect lighthouses and iconic lobster dinners, Acadia National Park is home to an astonishing variety of wild animals and plants. From tiny subalpine plants that cling tenaciously to windswept mountaintops to spectacular warblers that flit about the treetops for insects to tidepool marine creatures caught in their temporary watery abodes.

Stunning ocean shoreline surrounds the rocky mountains and coastal forests of Acadia National Park.

1

Glassy freshwater ponds carved by ancient glaciers echo with the mournful call of loons while reflections of bald eagles soaring overhead float in silent ripples. The pristine ocean waters bordering the park are home to numerous fish and charismatic marine mammals such as seals, harbor porpoises, and whales.

The main section of Acadia National Park is located on Mount Desert Island. The island is shaped somewhat like a horseshoe, with Somes Sound in between the two sides. Towns on the east side include Northeast Harbor, Seal Harbor, and the largest, Bar Harbor. Towns on the west side are Somesville, Southwest Harbor, Bass Harbor, and Bernard. About an hour's drive from Bar Harbor, a separate section of the park, the Schoodic Peninsula, is less visited but offers spectacular ocean views and quiet walkways. Portions of another small island in the park, Isle au Haut, are accessible only by ferry or mailboat.

Originally created as smooth path for horse-drawn carriages, Acadia boasts 45 miles of historic carriage roads that offer hikers, bikers, and horseback riders a gentle path through quiet forests. The Park Loop Road offers 27 miles of spectacular scenic views along the drive, which offers easy access to some of the park's most popular features. Rising 1,530 feet above sea level, Cadillac Mountain is the highest point on the entire North Atlantic coastline and, between October and March, the first to feel the rays of the rising sun on the East Coast.

It is highly recommended that you begin your visit with a stop at one of the visitor or information centers, where you can pick up a park map and learn about activities such as the Junior Ranger program and other events. There is currently a $35 weekly entrance fee for Acadia National Park; see the park website (nps.gov/acad) for current fees. The America the Beautiful—National Parks and Federal Recreational Lands Annual Pass is available, as is the lifetime Senior Pass for US citizens aged 62 or older. Annual Acadia National Park passes are available for $70. Permanently disabled persons are eligible for a free Access Pass, and active-duty military members and dependents are eligible for a free Annual Pass.

Although the park is open year-round, most visitor services are only open from early May to late October. Food, lodging, private campground information, and other services are available in the local towns bordering the park. During winter

Learn about Acadia National Park with the excellent selection of maps, books, and souvenirs available in the park bookstores.

and spring, the park shares winter visitor operations with the Bar Harbor Chamber of Commerce, located at 2 Cottage Street in Bar Harbor. You can contact them at (207) 288-5103 or visitbarharbor.com.

Nearby Nature-Related Destinations

Boat Tours. Most visitors to Acadia feel their visit would not be complete without scheduling a boat tour from one of Maine's many coastal towns. Several nature tours leave the harbor in Bar Harbor, carrying visitors to a chance of spotting whales, harbor and gray seals, and harbor porpoises. One of the most iconic birds that can be seen on some of the tours is the Atlantic puffin. Birders come from across the nation to get a chance to see these bright, clown-like seabirds. May through July, they nest on several of the remote Maine islands, including Eastern

Boat tours leave Bar Harbor and many neighboring harbors to search for whales, seals, and puffins and other seabirds.

Acadia and the surrounding Gulf of Maine are famous for the opportunity to see whales and puffins.

Egg Rock, Petit Manan, Seal Island, and Machias Seal Island (also claimed by New Brunswick). Check the Maine Office of Tourism at visitmaine.com/things-to-do/on-the-water/boat-tours.

George B. Dorr Museum of Natural History. This nature-related museum is located at the College of the Atlantic. Displays and exhibits highlight the nature and wildlife of the area. 105 Eden St., Bar Harbor 04609; (207) 288-5395; coa.edu/dorr-museum

The Oceanarium and Education Center. The exhibits at the Oceanarium are filled with native Maine species of fish and other sea creatures. The touch tank allows a close-up view of marine creatures that are not easily observed.

Vivid fish and native sea creatures are a super way to learn about the marine ecosystem.

Trails on the property wind through marshy habitats. 1352 ME 3, Bar Harbor 04609; (207) 288-5005; theoceanarium.org

Wendell Gilley Museum. Celebrating birds and art, the Wendell Gilly Museum displays carvings of birds by Wendell Gilley and other avian art. 4 Herrick Rd., Southwest Harbor 04679; (207) 244-7555. wendellgilleymuseum.org

Abbe Museum. The Smithsonian-affiliated Abbe Museum showcases the talents of the native Wabanaki people. The fascinating displays highlight the native people's cultural connection with the land, including birch bark canoes and sweetgrass baskets adorned with porcupine quills. 26 Mount Desert St., Bar Harbor 04609; (207) 288-3519; abbemuseum .org

The Abbe Museum highlights the rich history of the native Wabanaki people.

Stanwood Wildlife Sanctuary Birdsacre. Birdsacre, located in the gateway town of Ellsworth, has 6 miles of trails. In summer the nature center has displays of native birds, including those that cannot be released back into the wild, and other animals. Donations are welcome. 289 High St., Ellsworth 04605; (207) 667-8460; birdsacre.com

Tidal Falls Preserve. About a 40-minute drive from Bar Harbor, you will find a unique phenomenon on the Taunton River. About 2 hours after high tide, strong tidal currents rush in over the shallow rocky bottom in the narrow channel, creating a whitewater waterfall that reverses when the tide goes out. Frenchman Bay Conservancy protects this unique destination as well as conserving other critical habitats in the state. Hovering over the water, ospreys dive for fish, while great blue herons patiently wade in the shallows hunting for fish. Herring gulls squawk angrily at bald eagles, and kingfishers call loudly from their perches. This is a good place for tide pooling when the tide recedes. 72 Tidal Falls Rd., Hancock; (207) 422-2328; frenchmanbay.org

Green Lake National Fish Hatchery. The hatchery is dedicated to recovery efforts to return the endangered Atlantic salmon to rivers that flow into the Gulf of Maine. Open for self-guided tours; visitors can view information about the recovery efforts of Atlantic salmon, which once were prized as a common sport fish. You can see different ages and sizes of Atlantic salmon in carefully monitored pools. Trails are also available here. 1 Hatchery Way, ME 180, Ellsworth 04605; (207) 667-9531; fws.gov/fish-hatchery/green-lake

Lamoine State Park. Maine's forty-eight state parks provide the opportunity to enjoy the beauty of the Pine Tree State. Lamoine State Park is a 35-minute drive from Bar Harbor. Shorebirds love searching for worms and insects on the flats, and sparrows pop up from the tall marsh grasses. When the tide goes out, you can search for sea creatures left behind on the wide gravelly beach. 23 State Park Rd., Lamoine 04605; (207) 667-4778; maine.gov/dacf/parks/index.shtml

Down East Sunrise Trail. The Down East Sunrise Trail is an 87-mile multiuse corridor connecting eastern Maine and the East Coast Greenway. It begins in Ellsworth, the gateway to Acadia National Park, and ends at Calais south of Moosehead National Wildlife Refuge on ME 314. This is the longest rail trail in New England and runs along the Down East coastal area. The trail passes through natural habitats where you have a chance of seeing lots of wildlife, including white-tailed deer, beavers, wild turkeys, even moose. On the trail, outdoor enthusiasts can enjoy hiking, biking, ATV riding, horseback riding, cross-country skiing, and snowmobiling. The trail passes near or through several iconic Maine villages and towns including Machias, which has options for delicious food and comfortable lodging. For details, visit sunrisetrail.org and greenway.org.

The 87-mile Down East Sunrise Trail offers outdoor recreation throughout the year.

Public Gardens on Mount Desert Island. Besides the Wild Gardens of Acadia in the park, several beautiful gardens are open for the public to enjoy:

- Abby Aldrich Rockefeller Garden. Reservations required. Seal Harbor 04675; garden preserve.org/abby-aldrich-rockefeller-garden
- Asticou Azalea Garden. 3 Sound Dr., Northeast Harbor 04662; gardenpreserve.org/asticou-azalea-garden/index.html
- Thuya Garden. 13 Thuya Dr., Northeast Harbor 04662; gardenpreserve.org/thuya-garden/index.html
- Charlotte Rhoades Park and Butterfly Garden. 191 Main St., Southwest Harbor 04679; rhoadesbutterflygarden.org

Birding Festivals and Events in Maine

- Acadia Birding Festival. Mount Desert Island. American Legion Building, 22 Village Green, Southwest Harbor 04679; (207) 233-3694; acadiabirding festival.com
- Down East Birding Festival. Cobscook Institute. 10 Commissary Point Rd., Trescott Township 04652; (207) 733-2233; cobscookinstitute.org/birdfest
- Rangeley Birding Festival. Rangely Lakes Heritage Trust. 2424 Main St., Rangeley 04970; (207) 864-7311; rangeleybirdingfestival.com
- Wings, Waves, & Woods. Island Heritage Trust. 420 Sunset Rd., Deer Isle 04627; (207) 348-2455; islandheritage trust.org/wings-waves-woods
- Schoodic Institute at Acadia National Park. Serving the nature-curious year-round, the Schoodic Institute offers a wonderful variety of classes and work-shops. Some presentations are even offered virtually. 9 Atterbury Circle, Winter Harbor 04693; (207) 288-1310; email: info@schoodicinstitute.org

Birding festivals attract nature lovers from across the nation to view the abundant birds of Maine.

The Acadia Birding Festival is the largest of the four Maine birding festivals.

Beyond the Boundaries: Selected Places in Maine to See Nature

Maine Coastal Islands National Wildlife Refuge Complex. Composed of five refuges across the coast of Maine, the complex of National Wildlife Refuges protects more than seventy-three offshore island and four coastal areas managing colonies of nesting seabirds, including Atlantic puffins, razorbills, common murres, and other seabirds. The mainland

Corea Heath is a great place to see bog plants such as sundews and pitcher plants.

divisions are located in Milbridge, Steuben, Corea, and Gouldsboro. These areas are great for birding and botanizing. 14 Water St., Milbridge 04658; (207) 546-2124; fws.gov/refuge/maine-coastal-islands-complex

Quoddy Head State Park. After a 2.5-hour drive from Bar Harbor, the red-and-white candy-striped lighthouse lets you know you have arrived at Quoddy Head State Park, the easternmost point in the contiguous United States. The name Quoddy Head comes from the Native American Passamaquoddy tribe and means "fertile and beautiful place." Several trails begin here and lead through rich moss- and lichen-draped conifer woods with

Trails at Quoddy Head State Park lead to a subarctic peat bog heath where you can see plants typical of more northern ecosystems.

Spectacular ocean views await visitors on the Bold Coast of Down East Maine.

dramatic ocean views of Maine's rugged Bold Coast. From the picnic area parking lot, you can hike 0.4 mile on the Inland Trail and take the spur to the Bog Trail, which has a raised boardwalk providing a close look at fragile bog plants such as pitcher plants and sundews. This peat bog heath features subarctic/arctic plants such as cloudberry, rarely seen south of Canada. Keep an eye out for boreal chickadees and spruce grouse in the area. Bring your passport to visit Campobello Island, across the Canadian border in New Brunswick, just a 20-minute drive from Quoddy Head. At the Roosevelt Campobello Provincial Park, you will find another bog boardwalk. 973 South Lubec Rd., Lubec 04652; (207) 733 0911; maine.gov/dacf/parks/about/state_parks.shtml

Baxter State Park. In northern Maine near Millinocket, Baxter State Park borders Katahdin Woods and Waters National Monument. Many visitors to Acadia plan an extra day or two to drive the 2.5 hours north to this area, as it is one of the best places to see a moose. 64 Balsam Dr., Millinocket 04462; (207) 723-5140; baxterstatepark.org

Moosehorn National Wildlife Refuge. Covering more than 30,000 acres, Moosehorn has two divisions. The southern division is located in Edmunds, Maine; the northern division is located in Baring, Maine. The refuge protects important habitat for waterfowl, black bears, beavers, moose, and American woodcock. Refuge headquarters is located at 103 Headquarters Rd., Baring 04694; (207) 454-7161; fws.gov/refuge/Moosehorn.

Coastal Maine Botanical Gardens. A visit to the 300-acre Coastal Maine Botanical Gardens, the largest botanical garden in New England, is not to be forgotten. Membership benefits include free admission and reciprocal benefits at gardens across the country. The garden is located about a 3-hour drive from Bar Harbor at 105 Botanical Gardens Dr., Boothbay 04537; (207) 633-8000; mainegardens.org.

Orono Bog. Orono Bog is about a 1.5-hour drive from Bar Harbor. The 1-mile accessible boardwalk loop trail allows visitors to experience the unique plants and animals of a Maine bog. Information signs along the trail explain the various plants, birds, and other animals you may see along the trail. Sundews, pitcher plants, and graceful bog orchids grow in the bog that straddles the boardwalk. Tripp Dr., Orono 04473; (207) 866-2578; umaine .edu/oronobogwalk

Maine Wildlife Park. If you want to be guaranteed to see a moose, Maine Wildlife Park is your place. Located about a 3-hour drive from Bar Harbor, the park is owned and operated by the Maine Department of Inland Fisheries and Wildlife with a strong emphasis on education and conservation of native wildlife and natural habitats. Almost all the animals in the park are here because they couldn't survive in the wild due to a variety of reasons. 56 Game Farm Rd., Gray 04039; (207) 822-6460; email: mainewildlifepark@maine.gov

Rachel Carson National Wildlife Refuge. Established to protect important salt marshes and estuaries for migratory birds, the Rachel Carson National Wildlife Refuge consists of eleven divisions along the coastal areas of southern Maine. Trails lead visitors through coastal habitats where you may see unique species such as saltmarsh sparrows and New England cottontails. 321 Port Rd., Wells 04090; (207) 646-9226; fws.gov/refuge/rachel-carson

Safety Notes

Acadia National Park is a popular destination, drawing visitors from around the world to see and experience the spectacular wonders of nature offered here. Mount Desert Island and especially the town of Bar Harbor become congested with traffic during the summer. The maximum speed limit in the park is generally 35 mph, but in some areas it drops to 25 mph or less. This is also a favorite destination for bicyclists, so please watch out for them and give them plenty of distance. Perhaps the greatest distractions are the magnificent views. Allow time to pull over and enjoy the scenery, and be aware that others may be distracted by looking at the view and not at the road. Fog often envelops the roadway, especially at the higher elevations; please slow down in foggy conditions. Helmets, lights, and reflectors are required for cyclists. Boaters are required to wear personal flotation devices

(PFDs). Swimming is available at Sand Beach and Echo Lake Beach, but lifeguards may not be on duty.

Always let someone know when you go for a hike. Dress in layers and carry rain gear, as weather conditions can change rapidly. Falling trees and branches overhead can present hazards. Dehydration can be prevented by drinking plenty of water, and be sure to apply sunscreen to protect against sunburn. Do not drink untreated water from springs or streams—that seemingly clean water may harbor parasites, including *Giardia lamblia*, which causes severe diarrhea. Be aware of fast-moving streams. Do not turn your back on the ocean, as waves are unpredictable. Wet rocks and seaweed are extremely slippery, and falls are common. Some trails have exposed cliffs with steep vertical drops that can be extremely dangerous. Be sure to refer to a hiking guide before attempting any hike. Climbers in the park need to follow park guidelines and safety protocols.

Never feed wildlife. It not only is illegal but also endangers the welfare of the animal. Stay a safe distance from all wildlife. Although very uncommon, black bears do reside in the park. Most will avoid you if they hear you coming. If you encounter a bear, make your presence known by talking quietly and slowly back away. If the bear approaches you, yell and clap your hands. When hiking, keep small children by your side or at least within sight—pick them up if you see a bear on or near the trail. Ticks and mosquitoes

No matter how tempting, never feed wildlife.

are common throughout the park, so take precautions such as using insect repellent and tucking your pants into your socks to prevent tick bites that could result in Lyme disease or Rocky Mountain spotted fever. If you find a tick attached to you, remove the tick and clean the bite. See a health-care provider if you notice a rash at the bite site or become ill later. Poison ivy is found along trails; learn to recognize this three-leaved plant. If you come in contact with poison ivy, wash the affected area with cool water.

Conservation Note

Please leave wildflowers, mushrooms, and other plants where they grow. When hiking, stay on established trails and watch where you put your feet to avoid damaging plants. Especially in cliff areas, avoid trampling plants, some of which may only be able to exist in these special habitats. Report any suspicious activity such as plant poaching to a park ranger. Remember that all natural resources are protected in the park, including rocks and minerals. Please leave them for others to observe and enjoy.

Protect nature to sustain our natural environment.

How to Use This Book

Common and Scientific Name

In an effort to create consistent communication worldwide, each organism has a Latin name—genus and species—that is unique to that organism. Common names of families are given with the scientific family name in parentheses. In many cases, an organism may have many common names, often varying by locality. In addition, genetic research is rapidly discovering new inherent relationships and associations; therefore, the taxonomic status of many organisms may change with the new information. In general, organisms are listed by order, family, and then genus.

Photo Tips

Sharp focus is the key to taking great nature photos. Overcast days offer nice soft lighting for wildflowers and animals. In deep shade, increase the ISO or use a flash. Bright sunny days create harsh shadows, so stand with the sun at your back and point your shadow at the subject. A flash will add detail to the dark shaded areas of the flower or add a speck of light to the eye. Image stabilization capability will help stop camera motion. For more-advanced camera systems, shooting close-ups at f/16 with a flash will give more depth of field and stop motion. When taking wildflower photos, be careful not to trample other plants. Use a telephoto lens to zoom in on wildlife, and be sure to keep the eye in focus. Approaching wildlife can be unsafe. Never approach too closely just to get a picture. If wildlife changes its behavior in your presence, you are too close. Be respectful of wildlife, and remember that it is up to each of us to help protect the animals and their habitats.

Suggested Nature Hikes and Wildlife Viewing Areas

We have listed several of our favorite natural areas and hikes in the park. Hiking guidebooks such as *Best Easy Day Hikes in Acadia National Park* and *Hiking Acadia National Park* (FalconGuides) by Dolores Kong and Dan Ring are available in park bookstores. To help plan your visit, you can download the free National Park Service app through the App Store

(apps.apple.com/us/app/national-park-service/id1549226484) and Google Play (play.google
.com/store/apps/details?id=gov.nps.mobileapp&pli=1).

The following areas or trails are suggested for the general public and families who
want to see wildlife, wildflowers, and other natural features of Acadia. Some of the recommended trails are wheelchair accessible or accessible with assistance. Of course the park's
animals and plants may not always be where expected, so it is a good idea to first stop at
a visitor center and check with a park ranger about recent sightings.

Always maintain a safe distance from wildlife, and never feed wildlife. Do not pick
wildflowers or mushrooms or remove any natural or cultural objects from the park. You are
more likely to see wild animals during the early morning and evening, when they are more
active. To protect wildlife from pets (and pets from wildlife), the park requires all dogs to
be on leashes no longer than 6 feet at all times. They are also not allowed on certain areas
and trails. See the park website (nps.gov/acad/planyourvisit/pets.htm). Service animals
may accompany their owners to all park locations and programs.

1. **Sieur de Monts Spring Area.** Sieur de Monts has been called the heart of Acadia and is one of the best places to spot nature in the park. Located off Park Loop
   Road and ME 3, Sieur de Monts is a must for nature lovers, with an abundance of
   opportunities to see wildlife and native plants. Dedicated to George B. Dorr, Acadia's

Maintained by the Friends of Acadia, the garden at Sieur de Monts is a great place to learn about native plants.

first superintendent, whose vision preserved and protected the nature of the park, a kaleidoscope of colors awaits wildflower lovers at the Wild Gardens of Acadia, where native plants put on an ever-changing seasonal show. Maintained by volunteers and the Friends of Acadia, the Wild Gardens include more than 400 native plants in thirteen sections representing plant communities found in Acadia. This is a wonderful place to learn about not only the wildflowers but also trees, shrubs, and ferns, all of which are labeled for easy identification. Gravel paths wind through lush gardens where visitors can relax on benches and view the many birds that frequent the gardens. The free Island Explorer bus stops here, and you can begin your visit in the Sieur de Monts Nature Center, which offers information about the nature of the park. Several gravel and boardwalk trails lead from the garden, including the Jesup Path and Hemlock Path, which create a 1.5-mile accessible loop through a boggy forested area. Bring your binoculars to search for warblers, vireos, and barred owls that nest here. You can also continue the hike to see the Great Meadow, a significant wetland in the park.

2. **Schoodic Peninsula.** Leave the crowds behind and experience the outdoor splendor of Maine by visiting the "other" Acadia on the Schoodic Peninsula. Located about a 1-hour drive from Bar Harbor off ME 186, the entrance to the Schoodic Peninsula is located near Winter Harbor, Maine. There is also a ferry from Bar Harbor to Winter Harbor, where you can connect with the Island Explorer. Check the Downeast Windjammer Cruise Lines website (downeastwindjammer.com) or call them at (207) 288-2984.

Schoodic Woods Campground Ranger Station offers displays of the geology of Acadia as well as plants and animals. Check the bulletin board for park ranger programs and other events. The Island Explorer bus stops here. The Schoodic Institute works in partnership with the park, supporting the natural history and environmental research of the park to support resource management decisions. At the historic Rockefeller Hall, visitors to the Acadia National Park Welcome Center can learn about the park with interactive exhibits. Public programs and events are also offered here. See schoodicinstitute.org. On the campus, the 0.7-mile Sundew Trail offers great views of the rocky Maine coast. Even though sundews may be challenging to spot, keep your eyes open for graceful twinflowers and bluebead lilies in spring and goldenrods in fall. Owl pellets on the trail are evidence of not only owls but small rodents and mammals that did not escape the keen eye of an owl. Keep your eyes out for snowshoe hares quietly nibbling plants in sheltered areas.

Avoid the crowds by visiting the spectacular Schoodic Peninsula.

Schoodic Loop Road is a 6-mile scenic drive leading through spruce-fir forests to some of the most easily accessible scenic overlooks in Acadia. Photographers are well aware of this hidden jewel of Acadia and capture the rugged beauty of the Maine coast with stunning scenics. At Schoodic Point powerful waves thunder against the rugged coastline, sending sprays of seawater into the faces of visitors. To avoid being swept out to sea, do not to get too close to the edge or turn your back on the ocean, as large forceful waves can crash with surprising speed and strength. Here the crashing surf wears down the pink granite, exposing darker black igneous intrusive rock caused by solidification of magma. The plants along the rugged coast are sculpted by the wind, forming sloping shaped sculptures of jack pine and pitch pine. Crowberry and rose shrubs provide shelter and fruits for red squirrels and birds such as white-throated sparrows and juncos, while yellow-rumped warblers and cedar waxwings flit about in the trees gleaning insects. In fall, long lines of double-crested cormorants, scoters, and northern gannets stream south along the shoreline.

Just off the Schoodic Loop Road, Blueberry Hill has a small parking lot bordered with sweet smelling beach roses. Here you can scan the ocean with your binoculars for double-crested cormorants, common loons, guillemots, and common eiders. Along with noisy gulls, bald eagles are commonly spotted here. At low tide, the receding waves leave pools of water on the rocky shoreline, often filled with sea creatures left behind until the next high tide.

The only picnic area in Schoodic, Frazer Point, is teeming with birds gleaning insects from the trees. (See the "Picnic Areas" section.)

3. **Cadillac Mountain.** Located off Park Loop Road, Cadillac Mountain is typically on the "must do" list for visitors to Acadia National Park. Rising 1,530 feet, it is the highest

Ranger talks provide information about the history and nature of Acadia.

summit on the Atlantic shore between Nova Scotia and Mexico. From October 7 to March 6, this is the first place to see the sunrise in the continental United States. Breathtaking views of Frenchman Bay and the Porcupine Islands from the summit have drawn people here for thousands of years, including the Wabanaki people.

At the summit the scarred pink granite and erratic boulders tell the geologic story of the glacially sculpted land that once was buried under 5,000 feet of ice. The short trail at the summit is wheelchair accessible but steep in some areas. At higher elevation, subalpine plants are stunted due to exposure to harsh winter conditions. Balsam fir, white spruce, northern white cedar, gray birch, and mountain ash are found here. Bearberry, three-toothed cinquefoil, sheep laurel, and northern bush honeysuckle are common plants. In summer, the soft pinks of spirea, bright yellows of goldenrods, and lovely purple and white asters brighten the scene. Efforts are underway to restore damaged areas of the summit. Please stay on trails and be vigilant to avoid trampling any plants in this unique habitat. Slow-growing lichens are easily damaged by a hiking boot.

Take time to quietly enjoy the views from Cadillac Mountain.

In fall, you can join park rangers and volunteers at the annual migratory hawk watch.

Dark-eyed juncos, white-throated sparrows, cedar waxwings, and even eastern towhees can be seen here. Keep an eye out for red squirrels chattering from the trees and shy porcupines. Turkey vultures and bald eagles float overhead, while herring gulls and common ravens troll the parking lots for crumbs (remember, it is prohibited to feed any animal in the park). From late August until the end of October, Cadillac Mountain is a great place to watch the annual hawk migration. Park rangers, researchers from Schoodic Institute, and volunteers count the raptors as they soar by. You can see bald eagles, broad-winged hawks, peregrine falcons, ospreys, plus many other raptors.

Vehicle reservations are required from late May to late October to drive the winding 3.5-mile Cadillac Summit Road. The road is narrow, so please be aware of cyclists. Weather can change at any time, including fog, rain, and even snow. Sunrise is the busiest time to visit, and reservations sell out quickly, but daily options are also available. Beginning in late February, reservations may be purchased at recreation.gov well ahead of your visit; they are not available in the park. Make sure to download or screen capture your confirmation code, as cell service may not be available. In addition, vehicles must display a park entrance pass through the windshield. The parking area is often quite congested, so please be aware of pedestrians. There is no Island Explorer bus service on the Cadillac Summit Road, but you can check the Bar Harbor Chamber of Commerce (visitbarharbor.com) for other options, including Oli's Trolley (olistrolley .com). Recreational vehicles and trailers are prohibited. Restrooms are located near the gift shop. Drones are prohibited in the park, so please leave yours at home. Trails to the summit include the 4.4-mile round-trip Cadillac North Ridge Trail and the 7.1-mile round-trip Cadillac South Ridge Trail.

Forty-five miles of carriage roads offer year-round enjoyment in Acadia.

4. **Carriage Roads.** Thanks to the generosity of philanthropist John D. Rockefeller Jr. and family, 45 miles of carriage roads provide accessible access to hikers, bikers, and horseback riders in the park. The 16-foot-wide broken-stone roads were expertly designed to preserve the landscape and lead to scenic views. Signposts at intersections provide directions, and seventeen picturesque stone bridges span streams and roads. In winter, cross-country skiers enjoy the quiet winter wonderland along the carriage roads. Carriage roads are temporarily closed annually during the spring thaw, also known as "mud season," from March into May. This is necessary to prevent erosion damage to the gravel surface, so make sure to check the park website for updates. Generous funding from Friends of Acadia helps with upkeep and restoration of the historic carriage roads. In summer, Wildwood Stables offers carriage tours for visitors. Because of the popularity of the carriage roads, wildlife is best seen during early-morning hours. Everyone must yield to horses. Cyclists must yield to horses and pedestrians. Grab your binoculars and look for birds such as red-eyed vireos, black-throated green warblers, and hairy woodpeckers. Other wildlife to keep an eye out for are white-tailed deer, wild turkeys, groundhogs, and eastern painted turtles sunning themselves on logs in ponds. A map of the carriage roads can be found on the park website at nps.gov/acad/planyourvisit/maps.htm.

5. **Wonderland and Ship Harbor Trails.** Two hikes on the "quiet side" of Mount Desert Island are great leg stretchers to see forest and coastal habitats. Located between Southwest Harbor and Bass Harbor on ME 102A (Seawall Road) between Seawall and Bass Harbor Head Lighthouse, two parallel trails called Wonderland and Ship Harbor

offer pleasant jaunts with rewarding ocean views. A 1.4-mile round-trip stroll, Wonderland is the easier of the two trails, but there are some rocky areas and tree roots. You can see pitch pine on Wonderland Trail. Ship Harbor Trail is a 1.3-mile figure-8 hike that passes through a tall spruce forest. In moist areas, the elephant ear–like leaves of skunk cabbage can be seen along both trails. Other plants you can see include Labrador tea, cinnamon fern, southern lady fern, bracken, sweetfern, and hawkweed. Many birds can be seen along the trails, including brown creepers that build their nests under loose bark, chicka-

Sharing the wonders of the outdoors is a wonderful way to raise nature awareness.

dees that nest in abandoned holes in trees, and juncos that nest quietly on the ground. Along the coast, look for herring gulls, great black-backed gulls, common loons, double-crested cormorants, common eiders, and black guillemots. Eagles and ospreys soar over the open areas. When the tide is out, these are both great areas for tide pooling, but use caution on the rocks and be aware of slippery seaweed.

6. **Bar Island Sandbar.** The "bar" that gives the town of Bar Harbor its name is a 0.5-mile land bridge to Bar Island, which is part of Acadia National Park. The sand-and-gravel bar to Bar Island is only exposed from 1.5 hours before low tide until 1.5 hours after low tide, after which it returns to being covered by 12 feet of ocean water. Make sure to refer to a current tide chart before heading out. This land bridge is one of the most accessible places in the park for exploring tide pools. The intertidal zone is where the ocean meets the land, and when the tide goes out, pools filled with fascinating marine life normally hidden under the water can be easily viewed. The intertidal zone is a unique marine ecosystem that serves as a watery habitat for many animals, including starfish, barnacles, periwinkles, and crabs. Remember that

At low tide, enjoy the fascinating sea life in tidepools along the Bar Island path.

seaweed-covered rocks are very slippery, so step carefully and try not to damage any marine life. Wash off sunscreen and insect spray before exploring these fragile pools. Never use force to remove anything. Always replace organisms in the same place you found them. Always be aware of the waves, and keep a watchful eye out for the incoming tide. Located northwest of the town pier, access the sandbar from Bridge Street off West Street in Bar Harbor. *Note:* There is no parking on lower Bridge Street.

7. **Jordan Pond Path.** While sitting on the lawn enjoying the famous popovers from Jordan Pond House, you can see the bright white clouds reflecting off the clear, glass-smooth water of Jordan Pond. The 187-acre lake is 150 feet deep, the deepest lake in Acadia. Mile-high glaciers carved the U-shaped valley and scoured the mountaintops into rounded shapes. In the distance you can see the two rounded features known as "The Bubbles," along with the sloping form of Pemetic Mountain. The ground you are sitting on is a glacial moraine formed from rock and soil deposits left behind by the receding glacier. Accumulations of rock and gravel dammed the valley, forming the base of Jordan Pond.

    Jordan Pond Path is a popular 3.3-mile loop around Jordan Pond through a spruce-and-cedar forest with wooden boardwalks over boggy areas and footbridges. Some areas are rocky and some parts of the path have exposed tree roots that can grab your toes. As with most hikes in the park, sturdy footwear is recommended. Sedges, cinnamon fern, and black huckleberries line the path, while wriggling tadpoles and minnows swim in the shallow waters, darting under a protective log if disturbed. Dragonflies dart out from their slender perch to catch a passing insect then immediately fly back to the same perch. Loons and mergansers may be seen floating quietly on the water; overhead you may hear the shrill call of peregrines, ospreys, and gulls. Listen and look for many species of birds, including common yellowthroat, black-throated green warbler, blue-headed vireo, American robin, and downy woodpecker. Early in the morning, beavers may be seen plying the water with their flat tails floating behind.

8. **Park Loop Road.** One of the highlights of Acadia, Park Loop Road is a 27-mile paved road that passes through magnificent scenic areas of Acadia National Park. In summer the free Island Explorer buses are a great way to see the highlights of Acadia along Park Loop Road. The road and parking lots get extremely congested in the summer months. Speed limits vary but never exceed 35 mph. The entrance station along Park Loop Road is located near the intersection with Schooner Head Road. All vehicles must

display a park entrance pass. Once you enter Park Loop Road, it is one way. In some parts of the loop, parking is allowed on the right side of the road. Please drive cautiously and watch out for pedestrians crossing the road.

In spring, visitors can observe nesting peregrine falcons, back from the brink of extinction, on the cliffs along Park Loop Road.

Hulls Cove Visitor Center is a great place to start your visit.

Hulls Cove Visitor Center. Begin your visit with a stop at the accessible park visitor center. Here you can find information about the park and pick up maps and other helpful books to help you learn about the park. You and your family members can also find out about the Junior Ranger program in Acadia. Junior Rangers not only learn about the park but also promise to take care of Acadia. You will also be able to find out about upcoming ranger programs . The free Island Explorer bus stops here.

You can learn about the park by participating in the Junior Ranger program.

Sieur de Monts. A favorite destination for nature lovers, Sieur de Monts offers visitor information at the nature center. To learn more about the park's ecology and plants, stroll through the Wild Gardens of Acadia. (See "Sieur de Monts Spring Area.")

Sand Beach. Popular with families, Sand Beach offers an opportunity to experience the toe-numbing cold waters of Maine. Make sure to get a

A visit to the nature center at Sieur de Monts is a fun way to learn about the nature of the park.

close up of the "sand"—the beach is composed mainly of colorful crushed shells.

Ocean Path. The Ocean Path stretches 2.2 miles between Sand Beach and Otter Point, offering exquisite views of the rocky ocean shoreline. The concrete-and-gravel trail goes 0.7 mile from Sand Beach to another popular location, Thunder Hole. Beyond Thunder Hole, the trail is rocky with uneven surfaces. There are steep drops into the ocean and two staircases around a cliff. Watch out for poison ivy along the trail. Keep an eye out for common eiders and double-crested cormorants in the cold water.

Thunder Hole. When conditions are right, this geological wonder produces a loud boom that sounds like thunder. When the tide is high and winds are in the right direction, waves are compressed into a cave under the narrow rock crevice, then erupting with a powerful boom. Do not venture too close during stormy weather—people have been swept into the dangerous ocean. In winter, great cormorants can be seen here.

Otter Cliff. The spectacular 110-foot granite escarpment of Otter Cliff is a favorite with rock climbers. The rocks here show glacial striations, evidence of glaciers etching into the granite. Sea otters are not found here; however, watch for seabirds including double-crested cormorants, common eiders, and scoters. Black guillemots nest on the cliffs. In the trees and shrubs at the Otter Point parking area, look for small birds such as American redstarts, black-and-white warblers, northern parula warblers, magnolia warblers, and black-throated green warblers.

Jordan Pond. Formed by the power of glaciers, Jordan Pond is carved between Penobscot Mountain, The Bubbles, and Pemetic Mountain. Jordan Pond House rests on a moraine left behind by the glacier. (See the "Jordan Pond Path" section.)

Formed by the power of glaciers, the U-shaped valley is evident at Jordan Pond.

Cadillac Mountain. Cadillac Mountain is the highest mountain in Acadia. The two-way 3.5-mile road winds to the summit. Stay vigilant for other vehicles, cyclists, and pedestrians. Reservations are required from late May to late October to drive up the mountain. (See the "Cadillac Mountain" section.)

9. **Picnic Areas.** The six picnic areas in Acadia provide a quiet place to relax and enjoy the nature around you.

Thompson Island. Located off ME 3 just over the bridge from Trenton, Thompson Island Picnic Area has views of Thomas Bay. Some picnic sites are in an open grassy area; others are surrounded by northern red oak, white birch, and tall spruces adorned with beard lichen. This is a favorite stop for bird-watchers. When the tide is out, the exposed mudflats provide feeding habitat for migrating shorebirds such as greater yellowlegs and spotted sandpipers. Song sparrows search for insects and seeds among the shrubs and trees that line the edges. This is also a great place to see American redstarts, red-eyed vireos, and American robins. Butterflies flitting from flowers in the open meadow include American coppers and common ringlets. Salt marsh grasses create disheveled mini golden-brown waves where you can find numerous dragonflies perched waiting for an insect to fly by. Banded killifish dart about in the shallows. Here you can also see Ellsworth Schist, the oldest rock formation on Mount Desert Island.

Bear Brook. Bear Brook Picnic Area is located on Park Loop Road less than 0.5 mile beyond the ME 3 Sieur de Monts Spring turnoff. This forested picnic area has thirty-five sites nestled under mixed-forest trees of red oak and pitch pine where gray squirrels scamper through the branches. In August you can see bright yellow blooms of goldenrod. Even though you are not allowed to collect mushrooms in the park, you can observe many species here, including black trumpets, coral mushrooms, oyster mushrooms, and bright red–capped russulas. Amid the mushrooms you may see the white blooms of ghost pipe (*Monotropa uniflora*), which is not a fungus but a mycorrhizal flowering plant forming a complex life relationship with both trees and fungi.

Fabbri. Located on Park Loop Road past Otter Point, Fabbri has twenty-three sites. This is a great place to enjoy your lunch and the nature around you. Attracted to the numerous wildflowers here, butterflies including the large yellow Canadian swallowtails nectar at the sweet blooms. One of the "birdiest" of the park's picnic areas on Mount Desert Island, here you can see hairy woodpeckers nesting in round holes in trees. Numerous warblers can be seen here, including black-throated green and black-and-white warblers and American redstarts. Black-capped chickadees, red-breasted nuthatches, and golden-crowned kinglets flit about the trees searching for tiny insect meals. Dragonflies dart back and forth from perches in wet areas.

Pretty Marsh. Located on the west side of the island off ME 102 between Somesville and Seal Cove, the peaceful Pretty Marsh Picnic Area has eleven picnic tables situated under tall spruce trees. The silence is broken only by the chittering of red squirrels, punctuated by the toy-horn squeak of red breasted nuthatches, while juncos flit across the road when a car passes by. Look for winter wrens in the shrubs along the path to the shelter overlooking Pretty Marsh Harbor. In July you can see the pale yellow bell-like blooms of northern bush honeysuckle, hawkweed, and oxeye daisies. In late summer the rich woods team with mushrooms, including amanitas, coral fungi, and boletes.

Seawall. Seawall Picnic Area is located on the west side of Mount Desert Island off ME 102A, opposite the Seawall Campground entrance. Some of the fourteen sites are on the rocky coastline; others are in forested areas. This is a great place to spend some time relaxing at the ocean's edge and watching birds such as gulls, terns, and double-crested cormorants. Don't stray too far from your picnic table, as crows and raccoons patrol the area looking for any opportunity to grab a snack. Don't give into the urge to feed them—it is against park regulations.

Frazer Point. Located off ME 186 on the Schoodic Peninsula, Frazer Point is a destination for packing a lunch and your binoculars to enjoy spotting many birds. A small pier juts out into Mosquito Harbor, where you can see double-crested cormorants, black guillemots, and common eiders. In the trees and shrubby areas, you can see golden-crowned kinglets, red-eyed vireos, cedar waxwings, and even crossbills if you are lucky.

10. **Outer Islands.** Islands in the Gulf of Maine dot the ocean surrounding Acadia.

Baker Island. Baker Island is one of the Cranberry Isles in Frenchman Bay. In summer, the park offers ranger-led tours of the island. Here visitors can see flower-filled meadows attracting butterflies and other insects. The hike across the island leads to the ocean edge and a flat slab of granite known as the "Dance Floor." Keep an eye out for great black-backed gulls, long-tailed ducks, and bald eagles.

Isle au Haut. This remote island is partially owned by Acadia National Park. A passenger ferry from Stonington carries visitors to the remote island. There are few services available on the island, but camping is permitted at Duck Harbor Campground, where five sites are available in the summer. Reservations are required for camping.

Eighteen miles of trails lead through red spruce and balsam fir forests on the island. Visitors should bring all supplies and be prepared for changing weather conditions. Be on the lookout for double-crested cormorants; white-winged, black, and surf scoters; common eiders; purple sandpipers; and other birds.

Ecosystems

Acadia has been shaped by millions of years of volcanic activity, glaciers, and the constant battering of ocean waves. The park includes 20 mountains, 64 miles of Atlantic coastline, and 24 lakes and ponds. Acadia is in the transition zone between deciduous and coniferous forests, providing habitat for a large number of plant and animal species. In 1947, dry conditions led to a massive fire that burned more than half of the eastern side of Mount Desert Island, dramatically influencing the forest type. Over 20 percent of the park is classified as wetland, including swamps, marshes, and bogs. Some of the wetlands are fed by freshwater streams; others are saltwater marshes close to the ocean. These varied environments form the Acadia National Park ecosystem.

Once covered by a mile of ice, large boulders called glacial erratics were transported many miles by glaciers and deposited where they lie today.

AMERICAN BEAVER
Castor canadensis
Beaver family (Castoridae)
Quick ID: Glossy dark brown fur; rounded head, small rounded ears; broad flattened paddle-shaped tail; large orange incisors

Length: 3–3.9 feet   Weight: 35–50 pounds

Widely recognized by the large flat paddle-shaped tail, American beavers are natural engineers of the water world. Cutting trees with its large chisel-like teeth, the beaver constructs dams and lodges in streams, making its own private fishing area and home. Adept at conserving oxygen these aquatic specialists can remain submerged for 15 minutes. They typically swim with only their head and upper back exposed, leaving the distinctive flattened tail underwater. Beavers have a unique digestive system that allows them to eat and digest bark and cambium, the inner layer of wood under the bark. They have a symbiotic relationship with microorganisms in their intestines that digest cellulose. Valued by trappers for their pelts, beavers were extirpated from Mount Desert Island. In 1920 they were reintroduced by the "Father of Acadia," Geroge B. Dorr, restoring their natural place in Acadia's freshwater ponds and lakes.

WOODCHUCK
Marmota monax
Squirrel family (Sciuridae)
Quick ID: Brownish-gray heavy body; short legs; tail about 5 inches long

Length: 16–20 inches   Weight: 5–13 pounds

Hikers along carriage roads in the park are sometimes surprised to see a dark, rather rotund mammal nibbling on grass that may give a sharp whistle alarm call before quickly scampering off into the woods or down a hole. Woodchucks, or groundhogs, often sit upright, watching out for danger, and scamper to safety as hikers or bikers pass by. The voracious appetite of woodchucks led to the common name of groundhog, as they can eat more than one-third of their body weight per day and can often be seen at dawn and dusk feasting in lush grassy areas. Woodchucks dig large underground burrows that are 4 to 5 feet deep and 14 to 30 feet long. After fattening up during the summer, they head into their underground burrows around October to hibernate through the long, cold winter. In spring, when the warming sun melts the snow and ice cover, they emerge from their long sleep. The common name "woodchuck" may have been derived from the Algonquin name for this animal, *wejack* or *wuchak*.

EASTERN CHIPMUNK
Tamias striatus
Squirrel family (Sciuridae)
Quick ID: Small, reddish brown; one white stripe on each side bordered by black; broken creamy white eye-ring

Length: 5–6 inches   Weight: 2.5–4.5 ounces

Resembling miniature striped squirrels, eastern chipmunks entertain visitors to Acadia with their constant motion as they search for food. They are often confused with the park's slightly larger and much more vocal red squirrels, which lack the chipmunk's black-bordered white side stripe. Chipmunks tend to forage close to protective shelters, including shrubs, rock piles, rock walls, buildings, and cabins. Unlike many animals that are active at dawn or dusk, chipmunks are most active in the afternoon, when the stripes on their back blend well with afternoon shadows, providing them with better protection from predators such as hawks and the numerous ravens that patrol the ground for potential prey. During the fall they busily store nuts and seeds in underground burrows where they spend the winter in a state of torpor, waking about twice a week to grab a midwinter snack. The eastern chipmunk is the sole species of chipmunk in the eastern states, whereas wildlife lovers in the West are challenged with identifying numerous species of chipmunks. Look for chipmunks in wooded areas throughout the park, including Sieur de Monts.

EASTERN GRAY SQUIRREL
Sciurus carolinensis
Squirrel family (Sciuridae)
Quick ID: Salt-and-pepper gray back and bushy tail; brown sides; white underparts

Length: Body, 8–10 inches; tail,
8–10 inches   Weight: 9–17 ounces

With a fluffy tail as long as its head and body, the eastern gray squirrel has a total length of about 20 inches. The genus name, *Sciurus*, means "tail shadow," referring to the ability of a squirrel to sit in the shadow of its own luxuriant tail. Male and female gray squirrels are similar in size and coloration. The smaller red squirrels (*Tamiasciurus hudsonicus*) have reddish-brown fur and are much more vocal than their larger cousins. Gray squirrels gather nuts and hide them in many scattered places for the long winters. Each squirrel may bury a thousand nuts each season, some of which reseed, adding to regeneration of the forest. They have excellent memories and can recognize the location of these caches as well as use their sense of smell. Gray squirrels build a twig-and-leaf nest called a drey in the forks of trees.

Discarded cone scales

RED SQUIRREL
Tamiasciurus hudsonicus
Squirrel family (Sciuridae)
Quick ID: Small with rusty-reddish fur with black lateral stripes; white underbelly; reddish tail; white eye-ring

Length: 11–14 inches   Weight: 6–11 ounces

Visitors to Acadia delight in the antics of charismatic red squirrels as they scurry about in trees, chattering loudly when hikers approach their territory. Often mistaken for the smaller eastern chipmunks, red squirrels are bold and animated and lack the black-bordered white stripes of chipmunks. The genus name, *Tamiasciurus*, refers to tree squirrels known as pine squirrels. The species name, *hudsonicus*, refers to Hudson Bay, Canada, where it was first documented. Known by several common names, including pine squirrel, piney squirrel, American red squirrel, and chickaree, it feeds on the seeds of conifer cones, using its sharp teeth and nimble fingers to break off the scales to reveal the tasty pine nut. The flakes of the cones are left in large messy piles under trees or on rocks. Cones are stored in a cache from which the squirrel feeds during the long winter months. Red squirrels also enjoy mushrooms, often leaving bite marks in the cap. Put your detective skills to work and look for signs of red squirrels, including the piles of conifer cone remnants and mushrooms with bites taken.

DEER MOUSE
Peromyscus maniculatus
Mice, Rat, and Vole family (Cricetidae)
Quick ID: Grayish to reddish brown, white underparts; white feet; long bicolored tail; large beady eyes; large round ears

Length: Body, 2.8–4 inches; tail, 2–5 inches   Weight: 0.66–1.25 ounces

A deer mouse has a long bicolored tail with a very clear delineation between the brown upper part and the lower white part. Deer mice can produce from two to four litters per year, typically with three to five young. The young grow rapidly and are capable of breeding about forty-nine days later. An important foundation in the ecological food chain, these and other rodents are important sources of protein for a wide variety of predators, including owls, hawks, raccoons, and snakes. Other small mammals in the park include white-footed mice (*P. leucopus*), masked shrews (*Sorex cinereus*), red-backed voles (*Clethrionomys gapperi*), and northern flying squirrels (*Glaucomys sabrinus*).

NORTH AMERICAN PORCUPINE
Erethizon dorsatum
Porcupine family (Erethizontidae)
Quick ID: Brown chunky body, arching back; yellowish barbed quills

Length: 24–51 inches   Weight: 7.7–39.6 pounds

In a unique example of survival in the natural world, the hairs of the North American porcupine have evolved into an exceptional defense system. This slow-moving woodland inhabitant has a soft underbelly but defends itself with 30,000 barbed quills on its back and short tail. The waxy quills are tipped with tiny barbs that inflict a painful stab on the attacker. Once embedded, the quills are designed to work their way downward and, if they do not hit vital organs, may eventually exit from the other side. Contrary to popular myth, porcupines cannot throw their quills, but they detach readily when brushed up against a solid object. Native Americans in Maine polished the quills to remove the barbs and used them to adorn beautiful handmade boxes. Examples of this intricate handicraft can be seen in Bar Harbor at the Abbe Museum.

SNOWSHOE HARE
Lepus americanus
Rabbit and Hare family (Leporidae)
Quick ID: Medium-sized brown rabbit, white in winter; moderately long black-tipped ears; large hind feet

Length: 14.3–20.4 inches   Weight: 2–4.8 pounds

Snowshoe hares have earned the common name "bigfoot" for a great reason: They have very long hind feet and toes padded with thick hair, which allows them to travel easily on top of the snow. Their oversized hind feet help them stay on top of the snow, just like snowshoes. Perhaps the area's original inhabitants observed the snow-walking ability of the hares and learned how to fashion their own snowshoes to brave the deep snowy winters. Hares are born with fur and can eat grass within hours of birth. These changelings are speckled brown in summer but turn white in winter, which helps camouflage them against the white snow. As they primarily feed during the night, snowshoe hares are best spotted around dawn or dusk. In winter, you can recognize their tracks in the snow, as the hind footprint is in front of the front footprint. Look for these quiet hares in wooded areas such as those near Schoodic Institute.

EASTERN SMALL-FOOTED MYOTIS
Myotis leibii
Bat family (Vespertilionidae)
Quick ID: Golden brown to yellowish fur on back, creamy on belly; black mask; black ears

Length: 1.7 inches   Weight: 0.125 ounce

Burdened with an image problem, bats have been maligned as sinister flying rodents that will suck your blood and get tangled up in your hair. Although the Old English name for bats was "flittermouse," bats are not rodents. The wings of bats have a bone structure very similar to that of a human hand, with membranes between the bones. Unlike any other mammal, this special adaptation allows them to fly with agility surpassing their avian colleagues. Bats use ultrasonic vocal signals to find their prey. This echolocation enables bats to detect prey and avoid obstacles. Bats are essential to maintaining the balance of nature, as they eat up to half their body weight in insects every night. The eastern small-footed myotis is one of the most common bats in Acadia. Rearing only one pup per year, they roost in crevices or under bark. At dusk, you can spot these and other bats dive-bombing mosquitoes and other insects over Great Meadow.

BOBCAT
Lynx rufus
Cat family (Felidae)
Quick ID: Tawny to gray with black spots and bar; ear tufts; short, bobbed tail with black tip on top and white underneath; upper legs with dark horizontal bars

Length: 1.6–3.25 feet   Weight: 11–33 pounds

Although they are abundant in Maine, bobcats are rarely seen. Bobcats are crepuscular animals, active during dawn and dusk. Secretive and silent hunters, the bobcat's primary prey are rabbits and mice. While resting and sleeping, they seek shelter in hollow trees, rock piles, and brush piles with dense forest cover. With longer legs and large black ear tufts, the Canada lynx (*Lynx canadensis*) can be found in northern Maine where spruce-fir forests and deep snow are common. A visit to Baxter State Park and Katahdin Woods and Waters National Monument may provide visitors with a chance to spot these elusive cats. The much larger cougar (*Puma concolor*), or mountain lion, was historically found in Maine, but the status of any current breeding population of these large cats is not known.

COYOTE
Canis latrans
Dog family (Canidae)
Quick ID: Medium-sized, doglike; gray to reddish coat; pointed erect ears; long slender snout; black-tipped tail usually carried straight down; yellow eyes with round pupils

Length: 2.5–3.3 feet   Weight: 15–44 pounds

When natural balances are disrupted, nature has a way of filling in the gaps. In the East, habitat changes and the extermination of top predators such as wolves and cougars has made ecological niches available for the adaptable coyote, which has expanded its range from western states. Coyotes were first documented on Mount Desert Island in 1981. About the size of a medium-sized dog and with its black-tipped, grizzled coat, the coyote is sometimes mistaken for a wolf (*Canis lupus*), which is not found in Acadia. This hardy and adaptable canine feeds mainly on small mammals such as mice and squirrels s and will take advantage of carrion, especially dead animals on the road. True omnivores, they will also supplement their diet with plant materials, including fruits such as apples and berries.

RED FOX
Vulpes vulpes
Dog family (Canidae)
Quick ID: Small, doglike; reddish coat, white underneath; white-tipped, bushy tail; elliptical pupils

Length: 2.7–3.6 feet   Weight: 7–15 pounds

Both admired and loathed, the red fox has charmed its way into folktales as a cunning bandit whose sly character outwits both predator and prey. Using their keen eyesight, hearing, and sense of smell, foxes usually hunt in the late evening and early morning hours. Opportunistic omnivores, foxes will eat small mammals, birds, insects, plants, and berries. When food is abundant, they often kill more than they can immediately eat, caching the surplus under leaves or burying it for leaner times. Hunted for their luxurious thick coats, foxes have a relatively small body weighing only about 10 pounds. Like many animals that are active at night, foxes have a reflective layer of tissue behind the retina called the tapetum lucidum, which reflects any available light in the dark. Their elliptical pupils can narrow or expand to control the amount of light entering their eyes during the day.

BLACK BEAR
Ursus americanus
Bear family (Ursidae)
Quick ID: Large with black fur; light brownish snout; round ears; flat-footed walk on stocky legs; short inconspicuous tail

Length: 4–6 feet   Weight: 100–600 pounds

Home to one of the largest populations of black bears in the country, over 30,000 can be found in Maine. Even though bears can be found in Acadia, you would be very lucky to spot one, as they are not common in the park. Black bears are omnivores and eat a wide variety of plants, berries, and nuts, but they quickly learn that human food and garbage make an easy meal. To discourage bad habits, make sure to pack out any food or trash and keep such items properly stored. In the wild, bears typically enter their winter dens in November to slumber through the cold season. Emerging in spring, one of the early-blooming plants that bears find tasty is skunk cabbage. High in starch content, this odorous plant may account for more than 50 percent of bears' early spring diet. In fall, bears dine on sweet blueberries and nuts, including beechnuts. Unfortunately, beech trees in the park are suffering from several diseases, which may impact the ability of bears to store needed fat reserves for the long, cold winter months.

RACCOON
Procyon lotor
Raccoon family (Procyonidae)
Quick ID: Grizzled brownish-gray, stocky body; pointed snout; black facial mask, 5 to 7 black rings on bushy 8- to 12-inch-long tail

Length: 18–28 inches   Weight: 12–35 pounds

The distinguishing black mask across the eyes and a bushy tail with black rings are characteristic marks of a raccoon. The superhero black mask helps camouflage them during their nightly forages for wild foods, which include fruits, nuts, insects, rodents, and fish. They can sometimes be seen along the water's edge foraging for crabs, frogs, fish, and other aquatic prey. Raccoons are often seen near Blackwoods and Seawall Campgrounds in Acadia. With a magician's ability to open seemingly impenetrable locks, the nimble-fingered raccoon can open coolers and trashcan lids to rummage for tasty treats. In Maine, raccoons are known carriers of rabies, so contact with raccoons should be avoided.

STRIPED SKUNK
Mephitis mephitis
Skunk family (Mephitidae)
Quick ID: Black with 2 broad white stripes along back; large bushy tail with variable black and white

Length: 22–31.5 inches   Weight: 6–14 pounds

Skunks are one of the most recognized creatures of the animal world and are renowned for their defense mechanism. When threatened, these masters of chemical defense spew a stream of foul-smelling, oily liquid a distance of up to 10 feet, causing burning of the eyes and nose and nausea for the unfortunate victim. The genus name, *Mephitis*, means "noxious vapor." Mephitis was the name of the Samnite goddess of the foul-smelling gases of the earth, including swamps and volcanoes. Skunks forage at night for insects and plant materials and will readily get into unsecured food or garbage. Most predators will avoid these smelly animals, but skunks are preyed upon by hawks and owls.

AMERICAN MARTEN
Martes americana
Weasel family (Mustelidae)
Quick ID: Weasellike with pointed face and rounded ears; brownish; head and belly paler; buffy-orange chest or throat; long bushy tail

Length: 19.5–26.5 inches   Weight: 0.6–2.7 pounds

Commonly called pine marten, the American marten is a member of the weasel family. Found throughout Canada and the northern United States, they prefer conifer forests. About the size of a small house cat, this agile mammal is a treat to see as they move silently through the forests, often loping along a fallen log or racing up trees. Mostly nocturnal, this small predator hunts insects, rodents, and other small mammals. The closely related fisher (*Pekania pennanti*) is larger than the marten and is even more challenging to spot in the wild. The name is misleading, as these forest animals generally do not prey on fish but favor snowshoe hares, porcupines, other small mammals, and carrion. A smaller member of the weasel family, the short-tailed weasel (*Mustela erminea*), or ermine, has light brown fur with a creamy belly. In winter the coat turns white except for the persistent black tip on the tail.

Fisher

Short-tailed weasel (ermine)

41

AMERICAN MINK
Mustela vison
Weasel family (Mustelidae)
Quick ID: Dark brown fur with small white patches on chin, chest, and throat; long, slender body; short legs; pointy flat face; small, rounded ears; 6- to 8-inch-long bushy tail with blackish tip

Length: 12–16 inches   Weight: 1–2.2 pounds

In the same family as otters and martens, the American or common mink is a member of the family Mustelidae, which comes from the Latin *Mustela* for "weasel." Minks typically stay in close proximity to streams, ponds, and lakes and favor areas with protective cover such as rocky overhangs or brushy shrubs. Minks den in a protected place near water among tree roots, in a muskrat or beaver den, or by digging a hole in the bank. Their diet consists of rodents and other small mammals, fish, frogs, young snapping turtles, and snakes. Mostly nocturnal, you can sometimes spy mink searching for food at dawn and dusk. The same lustrous thick fur that keeps minks and other mammals warm in the winter has long been used by humans to ward off freezing temperatures. Historically, many cultures wore the fur facing inward for greater warmth.

NORTHERN RIVER OTTER
Lontra canadensis
Weasel family (Mustelidae)
Quick ID: Rich brown fur on upperparts with paler underparts; throat silvery gray; long, streamlined body; long, round tail with pointed tip; short legs with webbed feet

Length: 2.9–4.3 feet   Weight: 11–30 pounds

Many spots on Mount Desert Island contain the name "otter," including Otter Point, Otter Cove, Otter Cliff, and Otter Creek. Visitors might expect to see otters frolicking in the ocean, but sea otters are found only on the West Coast. However, northern river otters can be found in freshwater lakes, streams, and rivers on the island. Otter territories range from 3 to 15 square miles, where they may have several dens. Otters are famous for marking their territory with multiple latrines where they make a point of "doing their business" to help mark the pungent boundaries of their territory. Otters use their sense of smell and long whiskers to detect fish, amphibians, rodents, and other prey. Otters are very sensitive to environmental pollution and will seek more pristine conditions if necessary. Muskrats (*Ondatra zibethicus*) are smaller, with a thin, naked tail.

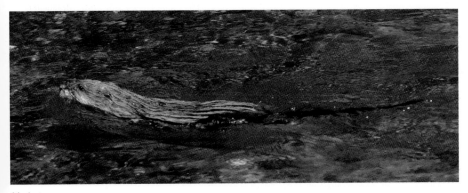

Muskrat

43

HARBOR SEAL
Phoca vitulina
Seal family (Phocidae)
Quick ID: Highly variable color from gray to brownish or blackish with dark spots on the back, creamy white below; rounded head with short muzzle; large dark round eyes; nostrils close together forming a "V"; lack flaps over ears

Length: 4–6 feet
Weight: 100–370 pounds

Also known as the common seal, harbor seals are shy but naturally curious and will often pop up near boats, to the delight of visitors to Acadia. Year-round inhabitants of the Gulf of Maine, harbor seals have

a rounded head with a short muzzle similar to that of a dog, while gray seals have an elongated muzzle similar to that of a horse. Along with their walrus and sea lion cousins, seals are in the clade of carnivores known as pinnipeds, which comes from the Latin words *pinna* ("winged") and *ped* ("foot"), in reference to their webbed feet. Often confused with sea lions, seals are more physically adapted to live in the water than on land. Their hind flippers angle backward, and they have stubby front feet, reducing their movements on land to a scooting caterpillar-like belly crawl. Harbor seals are carnivores, and their streamlined flexible body aids their expertise in catching fish, including herring, cod, and flounder; it is estimated they can eat up to 2,500 pounds of fish per year. Their natural diet brought them into direct competition with humans for fish, and there was a bounty on them for many years.

GRAY SEAL
Halichoerus grypus
Seal family (Phocidae)
Quick ID: Variable color from grayish to blackish with dark splotches on the back, paler below; rectangular horselike head with long nose; small widely separated eyes; nostrils wide apart forming a "W"; lack flaps over ears

Length: 6.5–8 feet
Weight: 330–770 pounds

Gray seals have a distinctive large, horselike head that helps identify them from harbor seals, which have a more rounded head. *Halichoerus grypus* means "hook-nosed pig of the sea." In males, called bulls, the top of the elongated muzzle is distinctively arched, or "Roman-nosed," giving them the common name of horsehead seal. With a straighter nose, females, called cows, lack the arched nose of the male. Gray seals are considerably larger than harbor seals and consequently were hunted for their blubber, meat, and hides during colonial times. Beginning in 1872 and extending about one hundred years, a bounty was placed on seals in an effort to reduce competition with the fishing industry. The growing tourist industry recognized the attraction of viewing seals, which drew tourists to the Maine coast. In 1972 Congress enacted the Marine Mammal Protection Act to ensure the protection of all marine mammals. This acknowledgment of the value of nature watching was perhaps a significant impetus for the current ecotourist movement, which supports economic interests as well as welfare of native animals.

WHITE-TAILED DEER
Odocoileus virginianus
Deer family (Cervidae)
Quick ID: Reddish-tan in
summer, grayish-brown in
winter; white around eyes and
nose; white throat, stomach,
and underside of tail; males
have antlers, females lack
antlers

Length: 3–7.8 feet
Weight: 147–297 pounds

Even though large mammals
such as moose and black bear
are not frequently spotted in
Acadia, white-tailed deer are

plentiful. Carriage roads and the Sieur de Monts area are great places to view deer, especially in the early
morning and at twilight as they come into the meadows to graze. Bucks sport antlers, which are shed in
winter and grow out again starting in spring. Lacking antlers, does give birth to fawns that are spotted with
white dots to aid in camouflage. Does often leave their fawns hidden under a shrub while they graze some
distance away to avoid attracting the attention of predators. If you happen upon a nestled fawn, remember
the mom is nearby and do not disturb the fawn. Please remember that even though deer may seem tame,
they are wild animals and can kick and bite. Feeding or hunting any animal in the park is illegal.

MOOSE
Alces alces americana
Deer family (Cervidae)
Quick ID: Dark brown, large, horselike; hump on shoulder; large "nose"; males have large, flattened antlers; females lack antlers

Length: 8–10 feet   Weight: 600–1,600 pounds

Representing Maine as the proud state animal, the moose is a recognizable symbol of wilderness. Moose found in New England and eastern Canada are members of the subspecies *Taiga* and are slightly smaller than Western and Alaskan moose. Male moose, called bulls, sport large, flattened antlers that average about 55 inches from tip to tip (Alaskan moose antlers spread 80 inches across). Female moose, called cows, do not have antlers and are smaller than males. Born in spring a newborn moose calf may weigh up to 35 pounds. Moose are unpredictable and can run at speeds up to 35 miles per hour. Use binoculars or a spotting scope to observe moose from a safe distance. Look for moose in areas with willow thickets and wetlands. Moose often graze on aquatic plants that contain concentrated sodium—an essential mineral in their diet. Moose are only occasional visitors to Acadia; if seeing a moose is a priority, your best chances are to continue north in Maine to visit Katahdin National Monument and Baxter State Park, where moose are frequently spotted. Ask at any of the information centers where moose have been sighted.

HARBOR PORPOISE
Phocoena phocoena
Porpoise family (Phocaenidae)
Quick ID: Stout body, dark gray on top, light gray on lower parts; slightly upturned mouth; black stripe from mouth to flipper; blunt snout; triangular dorsal fin

Length: 4.5–6 feet   Weight: 120–143 pounds

Harbor porpoises are small but fast and a treat to see in the Gulf of Maine, but you usually only see a bit of their dorsal fin. They often travel alone or in small groups, often making a loud puffing sound when they surface for air. The word "porpoise" is derived from the Latin *porcus* ("pig"). Harbor porpoises are often mistakenly identified as dolphins, but dolphins are sleeker, larger, and have a tall, curved dorsal fin. Dolphins also tend to leap out of the water much more than harbor porpoises do. To help prevent accidentally catching porpoises, fishing nets in the Gulf of Maine have pingers, which make beeping sounds that alert the porpoises to stay away.

HUMPBACK WHALE
Megaptera novaeangliae
Baleen Whale family
(Balaenopteridae)
Quick ID: Dark back, light belly; pleats on throat; small hump in front of the dorsal fin; underside of tail (fluke) marked with white

Length: 46–56 feet
Weight: 25–40 tons

Acadia National Park is surrounded by the rich waters of the Gulf of Maine, and visitors enjoy heading out to view marine wildlife with one of the whale watching tours available in Bar Harbor. The best time to see whales is June through August, during the peak season. One of the most commonly spotted whales in Maine is the humpback whale. Humpbacks strain small krill and fish through the baleen plates that line the roof of their mouths. You may also spot other species of whales, including the finback (*Balaenoptera physalus*), which is up to 80 feet in length, or the minke (*Balaenoptera acutorostrata*), which is only up to 30 feet in length.

49

COMMON EIDER
Somateria mollissima
Duck, Goose, and Swan family (Anatidae)
Quick ID: Males are white with striking black underparts and black cap. Females are mottled brown with barred sides; long sloping bill; sloping forehead.

Length: 24 inches   Weight: 4.7 pounds   Wingspan: 38 inches

With the exception of a few Muscovy ducks (*Cairina moschata*), which barely reach southern Texas, the common eider is North America's largest duck. The striking black and white colors of the male are easy to pick out, even from a distance. The male is also the only duck in our area with a white back and black underparts. The common eider thrives in the icy cold waters of the North thanks to the insulating quality of its down feathers, a layer of fine soft feathers underneath the exterior feathers. Along the rocky coast of Maine, they feed mainly on mussels and other mollusks, which they pry from underwater rocks with their strong bills. They also eat crabs and sea urchins, which they swallow whole. Look for eiders along the coast at Seawall Picnic Area, Schoodic Point, and at many offshore islands, including Baker Island and Isle au Haut.

COMMON MERGANSER
Mergus merganser
Duck, Goose, and Swan family
(Anatidae)

Quick ID: Male has greenish head; black back; white body; tapered orange-red bill. Female has chestnut head and throat; gray breast; white chin patch.

Length: 25 inches
Weight: 3.4 pounds
Wingspan: 34 inches

The common merganser is one of the commonly spotted ducks in Acadia. Common mergansers have an unusual looking long narrow bill with serrations that help them grasp slippery fish. In flight a large white wing patch is evident on the upper wing. The related red-breasted mergansers (*M. serrator*) are also found in the park. They too have a long, pointed bill, but males have shaggy feathers on their head and a cinnamon chest, white neckband, and gray sides. Male hooded mergansers have a bright white crest. Male mallards (*Anas platyrhynchos*) also have a green head, but mallards

Red-breasted merganser

Hooded merganser

have a flatter yellowish bill and dark chest. Female mallards are mottled brown, while common merganser females have a brown head with grayish body. Superficially similar to mallards, American black ducks (*A. rubripes*) are also common in wetlands and quiet lakes. In winter, boldly marked harlequin ducks (*Histrionicus histrionicus*) can be seen, especially near Isle au Haut.

Mallard

Harlequin duck

SPRUCE GROUSE
Canachitess canadensis
Upland Game Bird family (Phasianidae)
Quick ID: Chicken-like; dark mottled feathers; short, fan-shaped tail. Male is dusky grayish brown, black throat and upper breast; red comb over eye; chestnut-tipped tail. Female is rusty brown with brown barring on neck and chest; tail with rusty tip.

Length: 16 inches   Weight: 1 pound   Wingspan: 22 inches

An icon in the world of birds, the spruce grouse is the avian showpiece of remote evergreen forests of the North. The spruce grouse is one of the boreal specialties for which birders and other nature lovers travel to Maine in hopes of seeing. So quiet and camouflaged, this elusive bird is easy to overlook as it sits motionless on branches or on the ground while hikers pass by. Surprisingly tame, a folk name for this bird is "fool hen," as they were sometimes caught by hand. Unlike most grouse, which use their wings to produce sounds for their courtship displays, the male spruce grouse swishes his upper tail feathers, which catch on the feathers underneath. Their diet includes berries, plants, and insects, but they feed mainly on needles of pine, spruce, and other conifers. Some of Maine's birding festivals, including the annual Acadia Birding Festival, offer a chance for participants to see a spruce grouse in the wild. In Maine, the ruffed grouse (*Bonasa umbellus*) is lighter gray overall.

Ruffed Grouse

53

WILD TURKEY
Meleagris gallopavo
Upland Game Bird family (Phasianidae)
Quick ID: Dark brown body; unfeathered bluish head with red markings and wattles; brown tail with buffy tips

Length: 37–46 inches   Weight: 9–16 pounds   Wingspan: 50–64 inches

If Benjamin Franklin had his way, the wild turkey would now be our national symbol rather than the bald eagle. An important source of food for Native Americans and early settlers, wild turkeys were extirpated from much of the East by the early 1900s. Wide-ranging reintroduction programs were implemented, and today turkeys enjoy the protection of the national park and can be found grazing in the meadows and woodlands. At night they roost in the safety of trees. In spring, females may be seen followed by a line of up to seventeen awkward young, pecking at the ground for insects and seeds. The elaborate display of males proudly strutting for females is a dramatic show. Look for wild turkeys in open meadows and fields throughout the park.

COMMON LOON
Gavia immer
Loon family (Gaviidae)
Quick ID: Black head, thin dark neck; long, thin body, checkered black and white in breeding plumage. Winter plumage lacks checkered pattern and is dark above with white breast; greenish-yellow bill is daggerlike.

Length: 32 inches   Weight: 9 pounds   Wingspan: 46 inches

The iconic sound of the North echoes across lakes in Acadia when the common loon calls its mournful song. Park biologists keep a careful watch on loons in the park to ensure their safety. Listen and look for loons at many lakes and ponds on Mount Desert Island, including Jordan Pond, Eagle Lake, and Long Pond. In winter, when the water freezes, loons move to the open ocean along the coast or migrate to warmer waters. The double-crested cormorant (*Nannopterum auritum*) is another common large diving bird found in the park's waters. The cormorant is all black with a long snakelike neck and a hooked yellow bill. Cormorants swim lower in the water than loons. The less-common great cormorant (*Phalacrocorax carbo*) has a white throat. Cormorants can often be seen sitting on rocky outcrops with their wings spread out to dry.

Double-crested cormorant

Great cormorant

TURKEY VULTURE
Cathartes aura
New World Vulture family
(Cathartidae)
Quick ID: Black with silvery
flight feathers; bare, red head;
flies with wings in dihedral

Length: 25.2–31.9 inches
Weight: 4 pounds
Wingspan: 67–70 inches

A recent addition to Maine
skies, turkey vultures are now
widespread across the state.
They were first documented
breeding here in the 1970s.

Often mistaken for hawks or eagles, they even have the nickname "mountain eagle." Turkey vultures soar with their wings held in a shallow "V" shape called a dihedral as they search for food, using an extremely heightened sense of smell to locate carrion. They have pale silvery areas along the back portion of their outstretched wings. Look for them soaring along Park Loop Road and the west parking lot on Cadillac Mountain. Another familiar bird in Acadia, the wild turkey (*Meleagris gallopavo*) is not related to the turkey vulture but also has a featherless head.

OSPREY
Pandion haliaetus
Osprey family (Pandionidae)
Quick ID: Large; crooked wings; brown on top; white underbody and wings; dark mask across eyes; dark hooked bill; wings appear black and white–checkered underneath; flies with wings crooked in an "M" shape

Length: 23 inches   Weight: 3.5 pounds   Wingspan: 63 inches

Ospreys are large raptors commonly seen flying with crooked wings over rivers and lakes. Until DDT was banned in 1972, these birds and other large raptors were threatened to near extinction from the results of the pesticide thinning their eggshells. In full recovery now, ospreys typically lay two to four eggs in a large stick nest. In a fascinating display, ospreys often hover over the water, plunging down feet first to catch an unsuspecting fish. They carry their prey headfirst for less wind resistance. Skillful hunters, their success rate is about one in every four dives, with an average time of about 12 minutes. Sometimes confused with eagles, ospreys fly with a distinct kink in their wings that forms an "M" shape, while eagles fly with straight wings. When the alewife fish are running, you can get a close view of ospreys in action at the fish ladders beside the library in Somesville.

Sharp-shinned hawk

RED-TAILED HAWK
Buteo jamaicensis
Diurnal Raptor family (Accipitridae)
Quick ID: Large dark mottled brown hawk; broad, rounded wings; reddish tail; dark streaked bellyband

Length: 19 inches   Weight: 2.4 pounds   Wingspan: 49 inches

One of the most common hawks in North America, the upper red tail feathers can sometimes be seen when the red-tailed hawk banks gracefully on its broad rounded wings. Juveniles don't acquire the red tail feathers until they are older and instead have brown-and-white tail bands. The much smaller sharp-shinned hawks (*Accipiter striatus*) are long tailed and have brown to blue-gray backs with horizontal reddish breast bars. You can view these and other raptors during their fall migration. Acadia National Park rangers and volunteers from the Schoodic Institute count the number and species of raptors that fly past Cadillac Mountain. Migrating hawks can also be seen from Beech Mountain. One of the most numerous birds spotted in fall migration, the broad-winged hawk (*B. platypterus*) has rusty striped breast, light underwings, and three to four black and white stripes on a short tail.

Broad-winged hawk

BALD EAGLE
Haliaeetus leucocephalus
Diurnal Raptor family (Accipitridae)
Quick ID: Large raptor; brown body and wings; white head and tail as adult; yellow bill and feet; juveniles all brown or patchy brown and white with mottled brown head and tail

Length: 31 inches   Weight: 9.5 pounds   Wingspan: 80 inches

No introduction is necessary for America's symbol of freedom, the bald eagle. For visitors who have never spotted a bald eagle in the wild, Acadia is a great place to check this one off your list. Bald eagles are primarily fish eaters, and with an abundance of rivers and lakes, the park holds prime hunting ground for this magnificent bird. It takes a young bald eagle four years to molt into the recognizable white head and tail, so other large birds such as turkey vultures (*Cathartes aura*) and ospreys (*Pandion haliaetus*) may fool the eye. Ospreys are completely white underneath and fly with a distinctive "M" shape. Turkey vultures have a silvery look under their wings and fly with their wings held in a "V," or dihedral. Look for these magnificent birds flying past Cadillac Mountain, Schoodic Point, and at the nearby Tidal Falls Preserve in Hancock, Maine.

HERRING GULL
Larus argentatus
Gull and Tern family (Laridae)
Quick ID: Large gull; white with gray back and wings; wing tip black with white spots; yellow bill with red spot on lower mandible; pinkish flesh-colored legs and feet. Juveniles are brown.

Length: 25 inches   Weight: 2.5 pounds   Wingspan: 58 inches

Immature herring gull

The bold, raucous, laughing calls of herring gulls can be heard at every ocean-viewing spot in Acadia. Herring gulls are widespread along the New England coast, where they feed in diverse habitats including mudflats, fields, parking lots, and garbage dumps. Highly intelligent, they can be seen dropping shellfish onto rocks to break them open. It takes young birds four years to reach full adult plumage; until then they can be brown with various amounts of white feathers. The larger great black-backed gull (*L. marinus*) is the largest gull in the world sporting dark black back and wings. The much smaller ring-billed gull (*L. delawarensis*) has similar plumage to the herring gull but has a black ring around its yellow bill and has yellow legs and feet.

Great black-backed gull

Ring-billed gull

COMMON MURRE
Uria aalge
Alcid family (Alcidae)
Quick ID: Head, back, and wings dark brown; underparts white; white line on edge of wing; thin, sharply pointed black bill

Length: 17.5 inches
Weight: 2.2 pounds
Wingspan: 26 inches

Often described as a football-shaped bird, the common murre resembles a flying penguin but is actually related to puffins, guillemots, and razorbills. They can be heard vocalizing with a murmuring or purring sound, hence the name murre. In winter their throat and cheeks have extensive white feathers with a thin narrow line that extends from the eye onto the white cheek. Common murres were previously known as thin-billed murres to differentiate them from thick-billed murres (*U. lomvia*), which have a thicker bill. Many seabirds can be spotted on whale watching boat trips. Black guillemot (*Cepphus grylle*) is most commonly seen along the shores and bays of Acadia.

Common murre bridled morph

Black guillemot

RAZORBILL
Alca torda
Alcid family (Alcidae)
Quick ID: Upper parts black, underparts white; short stocky neck; flat, deep black bill with vertical white line; white underwings in flight

Length: 17 inches   Weight: 1.6 pounds
Wingspan: 26 inches

Yellow mouth of razorbill

Along with guillemots and puffins, razorbills are members of the Alcid family. Sporting neat black-and-white colors, Alcids, or auks, are superficially similar to penguins but are not closely related. Aptly named for their hatchet-shaped bill, razorbills dive hundreds of feet deep in the ocean to drive fish toward the surface, where they then grab the fish. In the mid-nineteenth century, it's closest relative, the great auk (*Pinguinus impennis*) became extinct; the razorbill is now the only member of the genus *Alca*. Razorbills nest in colonies on cliffs overlooking the ocean. A commonly seen black sea duck, the male black scoter (*Melanitta americana*) is black with a mostly yellow bulbous bill; the female is brown with pale cheeks. The bill of the similar male surf scoter (*M. perspicillata*) has a white patch with a black dot and an orange tip.

Black scoter

Surf scoter

63

ATLANTIC PUFFIN
Fratercula arctica
Alcid family (Alcidae)

Quick ID: Chunky; upper parts black, underparts white; cheeks grayish white; large triangular bill with yellow and gray markings tipped with red-orange; bright orange feet

Length: 12.5 inches
Weight: 13 ounces
Wingspan: 21 inches

The audaciously charming features of the Atlantic puffin have endeared this species to many nature lovers. Resembling clown-faced penguins, puffins nest in

colonies off the Maine coast, where they gather grasses to line their nest in a rocky crevice or burrow in the soft soil. Many visitors to Acadia come with the hope of spotting a puffin and plan to join a boating tour to one of the offshore islands such as Machias Seal Island, Eastern Egg Rock, or Petite Manan Island. Atlantic puffins spend the autumn and winter months in the open ocean of the Northeast but return to nesting colonies, where they raise a single chick, bringing it a mouthful of small fish to eat. In the 1880s puffins disappeared from their nesting islands due to overhunting, but successful efforts by the National Audubon Society and Project Puffin have helped reestablish nesting colonies.

Owl pellet

Great horned owl

BARRED OWL
Strix varia
Owl family (Strigidae)

Quick ID: Large, gray-brown back with white markings; pale gray facial disc, blackish-brown eyes, horizontal bars on head and neck; white chest and belly with vertical brown streaks; lacks ear tufts

Length: 21 inches   Weight: 1.6 pounds
Wingspan: 42 inches

Creatures of the night, owls are both feared and revered. The barred owl is a large owl with a rounded head and dark eyes. It lacks the ear tufts and yellow eyes of the larger great horned owl (*Bubo virginianus*). One of the most recognizable of all calls is the sentence-like call of the barred owl questioning, "Who cooks for you, who cooks for you all?" with the last syllable descending and drawn out. Their call sometimes sounds like a large dog barking. During the day, barred owls roost on branches and in cavities in trees. Hunters of the night, these owls have comblike structures on the leading edge of their flight feathers that break down the air turbulence and muffle any sound as they fly. They eat many kinds of small animals, including mice, voles, squirrels, and frogs. Barred owls may be active during the day and may

Snowy owl

be seen perched on a tree limb listening for the scamper of prey in the underbrush. Look for barred owls along the Jesup Path at Sieur de Monts and throughout the park. In winter, birders keep their eyes open for snowy owls (*B. scandiacus*).

Female

RUBY-THROATED HUMMINGBIRD
Archilochus colubris
Hummingbird family (Trochilidae)
Quick ID: Iridescent green back and crown; long thin bill. Male has a ruby-red throat;
female has a white throat.

Length: 3.75 inches   Weight: 0.11 ounce   Wingspan: 4.5 inches

This tiny hummingbird is one of the favorites in the avian world. Hummingbirds can beat their wings up to seventy-five times per second and zip in and away from their flower nectar source with the ability to fly backward and hover in midair. The ruby-throated hummingbird is the only hummingbird normally found in the East. The female has a white throat, and the ruby-red throat of the male can look blackish when not in good light. Lured by the sugary nectar of tubular flowers, the hummingbird's long, flexible bill contacts the reproductive parts of the flower, either picking up or depositing pollen and thus acting as avian pollinators. By early fall, these tiny jewels head south on their long migration to Central America.

Hairy woodpecker

Downy woodpecker

PILEATED WOODPECKER
Dryocopus pileatus
Woodpecker family (Picidae)

Quick ID: Large black body, white wing patch, white line on neck, large red crest on head. Male has a red forehead, red line behind bill; female has a gray forehead, black line behind bill.

Length: 16.5 inches   Weight: 10 ounces   Wingspan: 29 inches

The largest woodpecker in North America makes its home in Acadia. With a large strong bill like a jackhammer, they loudly drill a rectangular hole 8 inches wide and from 10 inches to 2 feet deep in dead tree trunks while searching for insects, including ants and beetle larvae. When seen in flight, pileated woodpeckers have a distinguishing large white patch on their wings. The word "pileated" means having a cap, or pileus. Two accepted pronunciations of the word are PILL-ee-ay-tid or PIE-lee-ay-tid. These strikingly large crow-sized birds can be seen in wooded areas throughout the park, but keep an eye out for them while hiking the trails at Sieur de Monts, Great Meadow, and Schoodic Institute. Other woodpeckers commonly seen are hairy woodpecker (*D. villosus*), downy woodpecker (*D. pubescens*), and northern flicker (*Colaptes auratus*).

Northern flicker

American kestrel

PEREGRINE FALCON
Falco peregrinus
Falcon family (Falconidae)
Quick ID: Large stocky falcon; gray barring; black cap; black moustache; long pointed wings

Length: 16 inch   Weight: 1.6 pounds
Wingspan: 41 inches

Once teetering on the brink of extinction, the peregrine falcon is once again plying the skies over Acadia. Due to effects of the pesticide DDT, peregrine falcon populations reached perilous numbers in the 1960s, but thanks to conservation efforts peregrines recovered and in 1999 were removed from the federal endangered species list. The population has increased steadily in the Northeast, but the peregrine remains on Maine's endangered species list due to low numbers. To reintroduce peregrines to the eastern states, in 1984 Acadia National Park participated in the first program by tending to a "hack" site on Jordan Cliffs. In spring and early summer, visitors can join park rangers and

Merlin

volunteers at the Precipice parking lot to see these awesome birds at the nest. During nesting season, trail are closed to protect the peregrines. Other falcons that have been spotted in the park are American kestrel (*F. sparverius*), merlins (*F. columbarius*), and rare gyrfalcons (*F. rusticolus*).

Olive-sided flycatcher

ALDER FLYCATCHER
Empidonax alnorum
Tyrant Flycatcher family (Tyrannidae)
Quick ID: Dull greenish olive above; two pale wing bars; thin white eye-ring; white throat; wide bill with black on top, yellowish on the bottom

Length: 5.75 inches   Weight: 0.47 ounce   Wingspan: 8.5 inches

Empidonax flycatchers are notoriously challenging to identify as to species. Alder flycatchers are similar in appearance to the eastern phoebe (*Sayornis phoebe*) and the eastern wood-peewee (*Contopus virens*). So similar is this bird in appearance to the willow flycatcher (*E. trailli*), they were once considered as one species called Traill's flycatcher. In 1973 genetic testing showed them to be different species. The Alder flycatcher prefers habitats such as wet thickets with alders, where it perches atop branches, flicking its tail downward and calling *fee-bee'-o* to announce its territory. *Empidonax* is Greek for "gnat" and "master"; *alnorum* is Latin for "of the alders." The olive-sided flycatcher (*Contopus cooperi*) sings a song that sounds like "quick-three-beers."

69

RED-EYED VIREO
Vireo olivaceus
Vireo family (Vireonidae)
Quick ID: Olive-green upperparts, white underparts; gray crown; white eyebrow, gray line through eye; red iris in adults, brown iris in young; hook on bill tip

Length: 6 inches   Weight: 0.6 ounce
Wingspan: 10 inches

Resembling large warblers, vireos have a small hook on the tip of their thick bill, which they use to capture insects. Unlike warblers, which are in constant motion, vireos tend to sit at a perch observing their surroundings. Quite an outgoing bird, the red-eyed vireo whistles a song that sounds like "Look-up-way-up-in-the-trees." These birds have a lot to say—researchers have counted male red-eyed vireos singing more than 20,000 times a day in the spring. In the same genus, the blue-headed vireo (*V. solitarius*) can be distinguished by the white wing bars and the white eye-ring and white line in front of the eye that resembles a pair of glasses.

Blue-headed vireo

Gray jay

Eastern bluebird

BLUE JAY
Cyanocitta cristata
Crow family (Corvidae)
Quick ID: Blue upperparts; gray breast with black necklace;
blue crest; white marking on wings and tail

Length: 11 inches   Weight: 3 ounces   Wingspan: 16 inches

Along with crows and ravens, blue jays are corvids in the family Corvidae. Corvids are well known for their intelligence, and their brain-to-body mass ratio is only slightly less than that of humans. Male blue jays are slightly larger than females, but other than that their appearance is the same. Blue jays are excellent mimics; their loud calls and sounds can fool even the best birder. Blue jays sport a pointed crest of feathers on their heads that may be raised and lowered at will and is often employed to intimidate rivals or predators. Acting as a public early-alert system, their loud calls alert family members and other birds to the presence of nearby predators such as hawks and owls. They will also engage in mobbing behavior, harassing unwanted birds, even hawks, that enter their territory. The eastern bluebird (*Sialia sialis*) is much smaller and has a rufous breast. A relative of the blue jay, the gray jay (*Perisoreus canadensis*), or Canada jay, is a northern species that you have a better chance of spotting in spruce-fir forests of Katahdin Woods and Waters National Monument or Baxter State Park in northern Maine.

BLACK-CAPPED CHICKADEE
Poecile atricapillus
Chickadee and Titmouse family (Paridae)
Quick ID: Black cap; white cheeks; black chin; gray wings with broad white edging resembling
a hockey stick

Length: 5.25 inches   Weight: 0.39 ounce   Wingspan: 8 inches

Often gracing decorative cups and towels, the charming black-capped chickadee is a nature lover's delight. So loved, it was designated the official state bird of Maine in 1927. Flitting from branch to branch, these busy birds glean insects, spiders, and caterpillars, stopping only long enough to wipe their tiny bill on a branch. Frequently announcing its name, the *chickadee-dee-dee* call is easy to identify. The call of the black-capped chickadee is slower and lower pitched than that of its cousin, the Carolina chickadee (*P. carolinensis*), which is found further south. Often traveling in small flocks with other birds, feisty

chickadees act as first-
alert sentinels, adding
even more *dee-dees* to
their call. They will often
boldly mob predators,
giving a sharp *zeet* alarm
call. Found year-round
in Acadia, black-capped
chickadees are regularly
counted on the annual
Christmas Bird Count.
Listen and look for these
chatty birds throughout
the park, including along
Wonderland Trail and the
Thompson Island and the
Frazer Point Picnic Areas.

Nest in tree

Brown creeper at nest under bark

BROWN CREEPER

Certhia americana
Treecreeper family (Certhiidae)
Quick ID: Slender body; streaky brown and white above, white below; long spine-tipped tail; slender decurved bill; buffy stripe over eye

Length: 5.25 inches   Weight: 0.29 ounce
Wingspan: 7.75 inches

So quiet and camouflaged, you may not notice this tiny bird until you see movement that looks like tree bark. Spiraling upward from the bottom of a tree trunk, brown creepers forage for insects, sometimes flipping bark aside with its downcurved bill. Their long, curved claws help it hook onto the bark as it braces itself with its long, spine-tipped tail. Once they reach the top of the tree, they fly down to the base of a nearby tree to spiral up again. The white-breasted nuthatch (*Sitta carolinensis*) and red-breasted nuthatch (*S. canadensis*) move down the tree trunk instead of upward like brown creepers. Brown creepers nest under a large piece of peeling bark, using sticky spider egg cases and insect cocoons to glue together small twigs and bits of moss and lichens to make a nest cup. Like many birds, brown creepers freeze against the bark when they sense a predator. Look for brown creepers at Sieur de Monts, the Ship Harbor Trail, and the Pretty Marsh Picnic Area.

White-breasted nuthatch

Red-breasted nuthatch

73

Ruby-crowned kinglet

GOLDEN-CROWNED KINGLET
Regulus satrapa
Kinglet family (Regulidae)
Quick ID: Olive-gray above, paler off-white below; two dull white wing bars; white eyeline; crown patch bordered in black. Male has an orange crown patch; female has a yellow crown patch.

Length: 4 inches   Weight: 0.21 ounce   Wingspan: 7 inches

Found in Acadia year-round, golden-crowned kinglets are very familiar with birders, who may have a challenging time keeping their binoculars focused on this bird as it flits through the foliage, sometimes hanging upside down as it gleans insects. Full of energy, kinglets seem to bounce about the treetops, chattering with very high *tsee tsee tsee* notes. When confronted or agitated, males raise their crown feathers to reveal bright orange feathers, while females sport a crown of yellow feathers. Along with its cousin the ruby-crowned kinglet (*Corthylio calendula*), golden-crowned kinglets often forage in small flocks or with "waves" of warblers, chickadees, nuthatches, and other birds. Typically hidden, the crest of the male ruby-crowned kinglet is red, which the female lacks. A good way to tell these two kinglets apart is to look for a white line over the eye of the golden-crowned; the ruby-crowned has a white ring around the eye.

CEDAR WAXWING
Bombycilla cedrorum
Waxwing family (Bombycillidae)
Quick ID: Grayish-brown body; crest on head; black mask edged with white; pale yellow on breast and belly; wings tipped red; yellow band on tail

Length: 7.25 inches   Weight: 1.1 ounces   Wingspan: 12 inches

High pitched and plaintive, the thin, high *zeee* call note of the cedar waxwing often announces it presence before you see it. Social birds, they typically fly in small flocks and gather at the tops of trees, gleaning fruit and insects before flying off to another feeding area. Cedar waxwings are soft grayish brown with a black facial mask and a cardinal-like crest that often droops over the back of its head. Their broad, pointed wings are tipped with red and appear to have been dipped in sealing wax, which gives these birds their name. Even their tail looks like it has been dipped in yellow paint. Their western cousin, the Bohemian waxwing (*B. garrulus*), has rusty feathers under the tail and white marks on the wings. Highly mobile, look for cedar waxwings throughout the park, including along the Carriage Roads and at Jordan Pond, Frazer Point, and Schoodic Point.

OVENBIRD
Seiurus aurocapilla
Wood-warbler family
(Parulidae)
Quick ID: Brownish-olive
back; white underparts
with rows of black spotty
streaks; white eye-ring;
orange crown patch
bordered by dark stripes

Length: 6 inches
Weight: 0.68 ounce
Wingspan: 9.5 inches

More often heard than
seen, the ovenbird is a
small, inconspicuous
bird that is quite cryptic
in the open leaf litter of

Hermit thrush

mature forests. Ovenbirds forage on the ground, turning over leaves with their thin bills as they search
for insects and snails. Its surprisingly loud rising call of "teacher, teacher, teacher, teacher" sings the
praises of educators. The ovenbird gets its name from its unusual type of ground nest. Weaving together
bits of grass, moss, and vegetation, it constructs a woven domed structure shaped like an old-fashioned
Dutch oven with a small entrance in the side. When alarmed or agitated, the ovenbird may raise its crest,
revealing the burnt-orange crown patch. If you happen to see this patch, it may help you to remember this
bird by thinking that it "scorched its head in the oven." Another unassuming forest bird, the hermit thrush
(*Catharus guttatus*) sings a loud melancholy song. It has a brown body with smudged spots on the breast
and a reddish tail.

BLACK-AND-WHITE WARBLER
Mniotilta varia
Wood-warbler family (Parulidae)
Quick ID: Black and white lengthwise stripes; striped crown; white stripe over eye; two white wing bars; slightly decurved bill; females duller than males, with a grayish ear patch and sometimes buffy on sides

Length: 5.25 inches   Weight: 0.37 ounce
Wingspan: 8.25 inches

Black-throated blue warbler

The high-pitched, squeaky *weesa, weesa* song of the black-and-white warbler alerts park visitors to look for this easily recognizable warbler. With a slightly decurved bill, these zebra-striped warblers creep up and all around trees and branches, probing under the bark for insects. They have an unusually long hind claw, which helps them grasp the bark as they search for spiders, grubs, beetles, ants, and other insects. The only warbler in this genus, *Mniotilta* means "moss-plucking" and refers to the bird's probing activity on trees. Sometimes observed in spring migration, male blackpoll warblers (*Setophaga striata*) are also black and white but have a solid black head. Black-and-white warblers can be seen at Sieur de Monts, Pretty Marsh, Cadillac Mountain, and Schoodic Institute. The stunning male black-throated blue warbler (*S. caerulescens*) has blue on the back.

Male blackpoll warbler

Female blackpoll warbler

77

Yellow warbler

Female common yellowthroat

Pine warbler

COMMON YELLOWTHROAT
Geothlypis trichas
Wood-warbler family (Parulidae)
Quick ID: Olive-brown upperparts; yellow on throat and upper breast. Male has a black mask bordered on top with white; females and young males lack the black mask.

Length: 5 inches   Weight: 0.35 ounce   Wingspan: 6.75 inches

As they hike by marshes and wetlands, most people hear the emphatic *witchity-witchity-witchity* song of the common yellowthroat well before they spot it flitting in the thick vegetation. If you stop to try to see this small, secretive bird, listen for a low *chick* call note and then try to spot its quick movements as it skulks from branch to branch searching for insects. The telltale black mask of the male common yellowthroat is a great mark to identify this small bird. However, the female lacks the black mask and is dull olive-brown on the top, with pale yellow throat. Widespread in its distribution, the common yellowthroat can be found from southern Canada to central Mexico. In 1766, a common yellowthroat specimen from Maryland made history as the first bird species from the New World to be cataloged by Linnaeus. Also brightening the edges of shrubby wetlands, the yellow warbler (*Setophaga petechia*) sings a *sweet-sweet-sweet* series of call notes. Pine warblers (*S. pinus*) have an olive-yellow back and wings with two white wing bars.

AMERICAN REDSTART
Setophaga ruticilla
Wood-warbler family (Parulidae)
Quick ID: Male is black and orange; female is grayish and yellow.

Length: 5.25 inches   Weight: 0.29 ounce
Wingspan: 7.75 inches

Maine is well known for its abundance of warblers, and nature lovers flock to the state to spot them. Flitting through vegetation while fanning its tail, the American redstart is a common warbler of spring and summer. The male redstart boasts Halloween colors of black and orange, while the female is dull grayish with yellow markings. These small songbirds are very active as they glean insects from the trees or catch them in flight in an aerial display called flycatching. The magnolia warbler (*S. magnolia*) has a yellow chest with dark markings and white spots in the tail rather than the yellow or orange patches in the tail. The "pleased-pleased-pleased-to-meet-you" call of chestnut-sided warblers (*S. pensylvanica*) can be heard in second-growth forests.

Magnolia warbler

Chestnut-sided warbler

79

NORTHERN PARULA
Setophaga americana
Wood-warbler family (Parulidae)
Quick ID: Blue-gray back with yellow-olive patch in middle; white underparts; yellow lower bill; two white wing bars. Males have bright yellow throat and breast with chestnut band on chest; females have greenish wash on back and head, lack chestnut on chest.

Length: 4.5 inches   Weight: 0.3 ounce
Wingspan: 7 inches

The high-pitched call of the northern parula is one birders soon learn as the rising buzzy insect-like *zeeeeee* trill that drops off abruptly at the end. The northern parula is a small bluish-gray warbler with a bright yellow throat. The female lacks the dark rufous chest band of the male. The name parula comes from the word "parus," which refers to another genus of titmouse. Pronunciation of "parula" varies from "PAR-you-la" to "Par-eh-la" to the accent on the middle syllable: "par-OOH-la." The similar Canada warbler (*Cardellina canadensis*) has a similar gray back and yellow throat, but it has all yellow underparts and sports a black necklace. Canada warblers also lack the two white wing bars of the northern parula. Palm warblers (*S. palmarum*) have rusty streaks on the yellow underparts and a rusty cap. Look for these and other warblers throughout the park, including Pretty Marsh, Sieur de Monts, and Schoodic Peninsula.

Canada warbler

Palm warbler

BLACKBURNIAN WARBLER
Dendroica fusca
Wood-warbler family (Parulidae)
Quick ID: Males are black and white with bright orange on the face and throat, large white wing patch; females are dull black with pale yellow facial patterns, two white wing bars.

Length: 5 inches   Weight: 0.34 ounce   Wingspan: 8.5 inches

A prize sighting for birders, the fiery orange face and throat of the adult male fill the binoculars with a delightful show. Blackburnians are challenging to see because they tend to stay high in treetops foraging for insects. Blackburnians have been spotted in coniferous forests in the park and nearby at Birdsacre/ Stanwood Wildlife Sanctuary in Ellsworth. To enhance your chances of finding blackburnians and other species, consider planning your visit to join one of the birding festivals, including the Acadia Birding Festival; Downeast Spring Birding Festival; Wings, Waves, and Woods Festival; and Rangeley Birding Festival. Monhegan Island is also well known as a great place to see birds in migration. Check out the Maine Birding Trail website (mainebirdingtrail.com) for more information.

Yellow-rumped warbler

Bay-breasted warbler

BLACK-THROATED GREEN WARBLER
Setophaga virens
Wood-warbler family (Parulidae)

Quick ID: Olive-green back; yellow face; two white wing bars; black streaks on sides; white outer tail feathers. Male has black on throat and breast; female is duller with whitish chin.

Length: 5 inches   Weight: 0.31 ounce
Wingspan: 7.75 inches

The black-throated green warbler is one of the most commonly seen summer breeders in Acadia. Its bright yellow face, black bib, and green back are characteristic of this lively warbler. The male and female are similar in appearance, but the female is duller and lacks the black bib of the male. In fall, immature warblers and some adults display dull brown and pale yellow plumages and are often called "confusing fall warblers" by bird-watchers, but the white wing bars are helpful in identifying this species. Another common warbler in the park is the yellow-

Cape May warbler

rumped warbler (*S. coronate*), which has a characteristic yellow rump. Lacking the yellow rump, the female bay-breasted warbler (*S. castanea*) is similar to the yellow-rumped warbler, but the male sports a rich dark bay color on the head and front. Cape May warblers (*S. tigrina*) have a yellow collar, and the male has a distinctive chestnut cheek patch. Look for these and other warblers gleaning tree branches for insects at many locations in the park, including Otter Point, Thompson Island, and Schoodic Point.

SONG SPARROW
Melospiza melodia
New World Sparrow family (Passerellidae)
Quick ID: Brown back; heavily streaked breast with large central spot

Length: 6.25 inches   Weight: 0.7 ounce
Wingspan: 8.25 inches

One of the most common sparrows in North America, the song sparrow is found in open fields and meadows. Their heavy brown streaking helps them remain unnoticed in brushy habitats. The diet of sparrows typically consists of seeds and grains, which they crush with their strong bills. White-throated sparrows (*Zonotrichia albicollis*) have a gray breast and a clear white throat with a distinctive yellow spot between the eye and the bill. The call of the white-throated sparrow sounds like it is saying "oh sweet Canada, Canada, Canada," while the song sparrow belts out a loud, bright song with three or four notes and then finishes with a complex melodious trill. Some birds, including the song sparrow, have varied dialects depending on their locality. The dainty chipping sparrow (*Spizella passerina*) has a bright rusty crown. To hear these and other bird sounds, check out the Cornell Lab of Ornithology website (allaboutbirds.org).

White-throated sparrow

Chipping sparrow

DARK-EYED JUNCO
Junco hyemalis
New World Sparrow family (Passerellidae)
Quick ID: Gray above; white belly; pinkish conical bill; outer tail feathers white

Length: 6.25 inches   Weight: 0.67 ounce
Wingspan: 9.25 inches

Deemed "snow bird," the dark-eyed junco is a familiar songbird in Acadia, where it can be found year-round. These common birds are numerous and widespread throughout North America, and taxonomists have been studying them and have described at least fourteen subspecies, which are

American robin

grouped into three large groups. The junco group found in Acadia is in the slate-colored dark-eyed junco. They hop about trail sides and open areas, feeding on insects or seeds much like the larger American robin (*Turdus migratorius*). Juncos often build a well-concealed nest on lichen-covered slopes, on cliff faces, or on the ground. Although not typically found as far north as Acadia, the eastern towhee (*Pipilo erythrophthalmus*) can be heard on Cadillac Mountain. Eastern phoebe (*Sayornis phoebe*) wags its tail up and down and announces its presence with a raspy *fee-bee* song, from which they get their name.

Eastern towhee

Eastern phoebe

Bill of red crossbill

RED CROSSBILL
Loxia curvirostra
Finch family (Fringillidae)
Quick ID: Crisscrossed bill. Males are brick red with brownish-red wings; females are yellowish with dark wings.

Length: 6.25 inches   Weight: 1.3 ounces
Wingspan: 11 inches

Sometimes in the ever-evolving world of speciation, seeming mishaps prove to be advantageous. The crossed bill of the red crossbill looks like an unfortunate birth defect until you notice how well these birds take advantage of their "deformity." They forage in small flocks, searching for choice conifer cones. Using their crossed bills like needle-nose pliers, they pry open the closed cone scale to expose the nutritious seed, which they grab with their tongue. Highly nomadic, these birds travel long distances to find suitable cone crops and are termed "irruptive," as they constantly travel to new areas. White-winged crossbills (*L. leucoptera*), which have two bold wing bars, can also be found in the park. Look for crossbills at Ship Harbor and Wonderland Trails, Seal Cove, Seawall and Frazer Picnic Areas, and the Schoodic Institute campus. Other reddish birds that can be seen in the park include pine grosbeak (*Pinicola enucleator*), purple finch (*Haemorhous purpureus*), and scarlet tanager (*Piranga olivacea*).

Pine grosbeak

Purple finch

Scarlet tanager

SPOTTED SALAMANDER
Ambystoma maculatum
Mole salamander family (Ambystomatidae)
Quick ID: Black with bright yellow spots; light grayish blue underneath

Length: 6–9.75 inches   Weight: 0.45 ounce

Although most visitors to Acadia don't see these quiet amphibians, four species of salamanders call the park home. The largest is the spotted salamander, which may reach a length of up to nearly 10 inches. They spend most of their time hiding underground or under fallen wood, but on a rainy night in early spring they may be seen traveling across roads or trails to breed in vernal pools. Females lay globular egg masses containing up to 200 eggs in these temporary spring pools, which lack predator fish that might eat the eggs. Long-lived, these salamanders may live from twenty to thirty years.

Aquatic adult

RED-SPOTTED NEWT
Notophthalmus viridescens
Newts and True Salamander family (Salamandridae)
Quick ID: Dark red spots outlined in black; aquatic adult green; terrestrial juvenile red-orange
Length: 2.25–4.8 inches   Weight: 0.18–0.39 ounce

Unique in the salamander world, newts undergo three distinct life cycles. They begin life in freshwater ponds as tadpoles. After two to five months, they metamorphose into a land stage. During this juvenile stage, they leave their watery home and walk into the forest. Now known as red efts, the colorful youngsters can be seen scavenging for invertebrates, especially at night after a rain. Their rough skin contains a powerful neurotoxin called tetrodotoxin, and their bright red-orange coloration serves to warn predators of their toxicity. After one to three years on land, they return to the water and enter the breeding adult stage as green water-dwellers. Newts may live for twelve to fifteen years in the wild.

87

SPRING PEEPER
Pseudacris crucifer
Treefrog family (Hylidae)

Quick ID: Tan, brown, or gray; dark lines that form an "X" on back; pointed snout

Length: 0.75–1.5 inches   Weight: 0.11–0.18 ounce

The high clear peeping notes of the spring peeper signal the end of winter and the return of spring. Although they are only about an inch long, spring peepers can produce a chorus so loud it can be heard over a mile away. Rarely seen, as they are often in trees, these tiny frogs have a distinguishing "X" mark on their backs. They are especially easy to hear due to their extremely loud mating call, which gives them the name "peeper," but it is often hard to pinpoint the source of the sound, especially when many are peeping at once. Peepers generally like to breed when it is closer to dusk and throughout the evening and early morning hours.

AMERICAN BULLFROG
Lithobates catesbeianus
True frog family (Ranidae)
Quick ID: Large frog; olive-green with or without gray or brown markings; underside creamy white; throat yellowish on males, whitish on females; lacks ridges on the back; eardrum larger than eye

Length: 3.6–8 inches
Weight: 6–12 ounces

The deep booming "Jug o'rum" call of the bullfrog is a familiar sound in wetlands, streams, and ponds in Maine. Native to the eastern states, the American bullfrog is the largest frog in the United States. At the frog buffet in wetlands, bullfrogs are ambush predators that will eat anything they can catch, including insects and other invertebrates, fish, and other frogs. Unlike several other frogs in the park, bullfrogs lack ridges on their back. The eardrum, called a tympanum, is twice the size of the eye. Females lay up to 20,000 eggs in large floating masses. Bullfrogs can take two to three years to fully transform from the tadpole stage. The large dark green-to-black tadpoles, or polliwogs, can reach up to 6 inches long and have a distinctive dorsal fin on their tail. Bullfrogs produce a high concentration of glucose during winter, which prevents their vital organs from freezing under the ice.

NORTHERN GREEN FROG
Lithobates clamitans
True frog family (Ranidae)
Quick ID: Green to brownish with darker mottling or spots on the back, two ridges extending along the back; belly white to grayish; throat dusky or yellowish; horizontal black bands across the hind legs

Length: 2–4 inches   Weight: 1–3 ounces

Acadia's ponds and lakes often resound with the well-known *jug o'rum* call of bullfrogs. But when visitors hear the twang of a banjo-like sound coming from the water's edge, they find it hard to believe that the call is coming from a frog, the green frog. Their trademark *glunk* call sounds like a plucked banjo string or rubber band. The green frog and the bullfrog are the most common frogs in the park. The green frog can be distinguished from the bullfrog by the distinct ridges along each side of the back, which are lacking on the bullfrog. The tadpoles are olive green and about 2.5 inches long. Two other frogs that can be found in the park are the wood frog (*L. sylvaticus*) and the pickerel frog (*L. palustris*). Only one species of toad, the American toad (*Anaxyrus americanus*), is found in Acadia.

Wood frog

Pickerel frog

American toad

EASTERN SNAPPING TURTLE
Chelydra serpentina
Snapping Turtle family (Chelydridae)
Quick ID: Brownish overall; flattened upper shell (carapace) with ridges; long saw-toothed tail; large head with blunt protruding snout and hooked jaw

Length: Shell 8–19 inches   Weight: 10–35 pounds

Ancient reptiles, snapping turtles date back 65 million years ago, and these primitive looking but powerful creatures live in the ponds, streams, and lakes of Acadia. Snappers often bury themselves in the mud with only their nostrils and eyes exposed, waiting for a passing meal of fish, frogs, crayfish, insects, or even ducks and muskrats. These turtles have powerful hooked jaws that they employ with lightning-fast speed. They have long, flexible necks and can easily reach beside their shell. The average weight is between 10 and 35 pounds, but the record holder weighed in at 75 pounds. Snappers long provided native Maine families with the primary ingredient for turtle soup, and their shells were used as containers. Eastern painted turtles (*Chrysemys picta*) are much smaller and can often be seen sunning themselves on a log near water. Look for these turtles at Sieur du Monts and at other wetlands, ponds, and lakes.

EASTERN PAINTED TURTLE
Chrysemys picta
Pond, Marsh, and Box Turtle family (Emydidae)
Quick ID: Upper side of the shell (carapace) dark olive, highlighted by smooth plates (scutes) separated by light colored seams; head, tail, and legs striped with red and yellow markings; head with two yellow spots

Length: 4–6 inches   Weight: 11–18 ounces

Of the two species of turtles found in Acadia, the eastern painted turtle is the one that visitors see most often. The much larger snapping turtle is not easily confused with the painted turtle. Painted turtles enjoy sunning themselves on half-submerged logs and rocks in ponds and lakes but quickly slide into the water if disturbed, revealing their yellowish undersides. The painted turtle is the most widespread native turtle in North America and is easily identified by the straight rows of large smooth scutes across the back lined with yellowish seams. The genus name, *Chrysemys*, is from the Greek words *chrysos*, meaning "gold" (referring to the yellowish underside, or plastron), and *emys*, meaning an aquatic turtle. The species name, *pictus*, is from Latin and means "to paint." The eastern painted turtle is the official reptile of the nearby state of Vermont.

EASTERN GARTER SNAKE
Thamnophis sirtalis
Colubrid family (Colubridae)
Quick ID: Olive green to brown; one yellowish-white longitudinal stripe down the back with a lateral stripe on each side; large round eyes with round pupils

Length: 18–26 inches   Weight: Average 5.3 ounces

One of five species of snakes found in Acadia, the eastern garter snake (sometimes called garden snake) is one of the most commonly seen. The genus, *Thamnophis*, comes from the Greek words *thamnos* ("bush") and *ophio* ("snake"). The species name, *sirtalis*, is Latin and means "like a garter." Garter snakes are so called either from the striped garters men used to hold up their socks or from a mispronunciation of the German word for garden. If disturbed, these snakes discharge a musk scent from a gland to discourage predators such as hawks, crows, and raccoons. Like any animal, garter snakes will bite if provoked, but they will typically try to hide or escape the threat. Garter snakes play an important role in the ecosystem, as they prey on rodents, insects, and slugs that damage gardens and crops. Other snakes that may be found in the park are the eastern milk snake (*Lampropeltis triangulum*), smooth green snake (*Opheodrys vernalis*), redbelly snake (*Storeria occipitomaculata*), and ringneck snake (*Diadophis punctatus*). There are no venomous snakes in the park.

AMERICAN COMMON EEL
Anguilla rostrata
Freshwater Eel family (Anguillidae)
Quick ID: Snakelike fish; gray to greenish yellow to brownish; long dorsal fin; pointed tail

Length: 2–4 feet   Weight: Up to 9 pounds

The snakelike appearance and slimy body of the American eel cause some anglers to reject this unusual fish, but historically eel was served regularly on the dinner table. A staple food for Native Americans, eels were roasted, smoked, and dried for use during the cold winter months. Eels have a fascinating life history, beginning life as eggs near the Bahamas in the Sargasso Sea. They metamorphose as they float on ocean currents until they reach the eastern shore of North America and find their way into freshwater streams such as those in Acadia. Eels hide in mud during the day and forage in the evening. Eels can absorb oxygen through their skin, enabling them to travel over land on moist evenings. Adults may remain in rivers and ponds for as long as fifteen years before returning to the ocean to spawn.

ALEWIFE

Alosa pseudoharengus
Herring, Shad, Sardine, and
Menhaden family (Clupeidae)
Quick ID: Silvery with grayish-
green back and one small dark
shoulder spot; body laterally
compressed and deep; ventral
scutes; caudal fin forked; large
eyes

Length: 3–14 inches
Weight: 4 pounds

Also known as river herring,
alewives are anadromous fish
that spend most of their lives
in the open ocean but return
to inland rivers and streams to

Herring gull with alewife

spawn. This annual migration typically occurs mid-May to mid-June, bringing these fish back to their natal waters.

In the 1700s, dams were built to support commercial efforts such as sawmills, gristmills, and woolen mills, effectively blocking the migration of these and other fish back to their spawning grounds. In 2006 conservation efforts resulted in the building of fish ladders to allow alewives and other fish to return in numbers to their native waters. You can see the effectiveness of fish ladders in Somesville Mill Pond on ME 102 on Mount Desert Island. These small bony fish are smoked or salted and are also used in pet food or fish meal. In Maine they are valued as bait for lobsters and large fish such as halibut. An important member of the food chain, alewives are food for many animals, including whales, otters, mink, and ospreys. In reference to the large abdomen of these fish, the name alewife is derived from the word used in medieval Europe for well-fed female ale brewers.

EASTERN BROOK TROUT
Salvelinus fontinalis
Trout family (Salmonidae)
Quick ID: Dark olive green to brown; cream wavy lines (vermiculations) on back and head; sides with pale spots and red spots with bluish halos; bottom fins white-edged

Length: 5–20 inches   Weight: 2.2–13.2 pounds

Maine is well known to anglers for its cool, clear waters that are home to native eastern brook trout. With ideal conditions for brook trout, Maine boasts more of an abundance of these fish than any other state on the East Coast. Trout prefer cold water, between 50°F and 65°F, with sufficient dissolved oxygen, such as those found in the streams and lakes in Acadia.

Pulling in a "squaretail," as they are commonly called in Maine, is a delight for anglers, but catch-and-release practices are preferred to allow these natives to survive in the wild. You can find brook trout in ponds including Upper and Lower Hadlock, Bubble, Half Moon, and Long, as well as Eagle and Echo Lakes. Besides Atlantic salmon (*Salmo salar*), other fish in this family found in the park include lake trout (*Salvelinus namaycush*) and brown trout (*Salmo trutta*). A valid Maine fishing license is required to fish in Acadia National Park, so make sure to check the laws and regulations on the website at nps.gov/acad/planyourvisit/fishing.htm.

Brown trout

Lake trout

Key Features of Trout in Acadia National Park

Trout Species	Description
Lake	Dark greenish with light-colored spots; deeply forked tail
Brown	Large, dense; black and red spots from tail to head with some on gill covers
Brook	Red spots with blue halos on sides, as well as light spots (topside spots are wavy); fins edged with white

ATLANTIC SALMON
Salmo salar
Trout, Salmon, and Whitefish
family (Salmonidae)
Quick ID: Tapered at each end;
silvery with some black spots
on upper parts; single dorsal
fin; adipose fin not black-edged;
unspotted tail

Length: 28–30 inches
Weight: 8–12 pounds

Highly prized as a game fish, the
Atlantic salmon was once known
as the "King of Fish." Historically,
Atlantic salmon were born in

freshwater rivers then migrated to the ocean. Atlantic salmon are anadromous, spending two to three
years in the Atlantic Ocean, after which the adults return to the rivers in which they were born to spawn.
A subspecies of Atlantic salmon, landlocked salmon (*Salmo salar sebago*), never migrate to the ocean,
living their entire lives in freshwater lakes. In 1969 the landlocked salmon was designated the official state
fish of Maine. By the mid-1800s, overfishing, pollution, and the construction of dams nearly exterminated
the population of these trophy fish in Maine. Since 2000, Atlantic salmon have been protected under the
Endangered Species Act, and fishing for them is prohibited in the United States. Conservation efforts are
ongoing to protect and restore this special native fish. Located about 30 minutes from Mount Desert Island,
the Green Lake National Fish Hatchery in Ellsworth is a great place to visit to see the valuable work of
biologists dedicated to these recovery efforts. Their website is fws.gov/fish-hatchery/green-lake.

BANDED KILLIFISH
Fundulus diaphanus
Topminnow family (Fundulidae)
Quick ID: Narrow, elongated bluish-gray body with lighter underparts; greenish-brown vertical bands on sides; silvery-blue cheek; large eye; slightly rounded tail

Length: 2–3 inches   Weight: Less than 1 ounce

Twenty-nine species of freshwater fish can be found in Acadia, about half of which are native to these waters. Many of these aquatic inhabitants are small "minnows" that serve as an important link in the food chain. One of these small fish, the banded killifish, is native to New England and is the only freshwater killifish found in the northeastern states. Killifish are able to survive in numerous aquatic environments, which is advantageous for their survival. They can sometimes be seen in shallow edges of ponds and lakes in Acadia. The word "killifish" is said to be derived from the Dutch word *kil* or *kill*, which means a small stream. Other small fish common to Acadia lakes and ponds are the golden shiner (*Notemigonus crysoleucas*), sticklebacks (*Pungitius* spp.), and northern redbelly dace (*Chrosomus eos*).

Golden shiner

Stickleback

Northern redbelly dace

PUMPKINSEED
Lepomis gibbosus
Sunfish family (Centrarchidae)
Quick ID: Laterally compressed body with greenish-yellow sides, mottled with orange and blue-green; yellowish belly; wavy bluish lines on cheek; white-rimmed black earflap with red crescent; spines in dorsal fin

Length: 6–10 inches
Weight: 6–16 ounces

Pumpkinseeds, or common sunfish, have a flat round body that is shaped somewhat like a pumpkin seed, inspiring its common name. These brightly colored sunfish are native to New England and have been

Redbreast sunfish

introduced into states south and west of Maine. They prefer shorelines where there is plenty of vegetation for cover. Although these small fish do not provide large amounts of edible meat, they are commonly known as panfish, as they are the perfect size for the frying pan. The redbreast sunfish (*L. auritus*), a similar fish that lacks a red mark on the earflap, or operculum, also can be found in the park.

CANADIAN TIGER SWALLOWTAIL
Papilio canadensis
Swallowtail family (Papilionidae)
Quick ID: Yellow with broad vertical black stripes; blue and orange markings on hind wings

Wingspan: 2.6–3.1 inches   Flight season: May–July

The Canadian tiger swallowtail may have an identity crisis, as many people confuse it with the related eastern tiger swallowtail (*P. glaucus*). Although they are very similar, the Canadian tiger swallowtail is smaller than its relative and can survive the colder northern climate. The Canadian tiger swallowtail also has a semisolid yellow band along the underside of the forewing margin; the eastern tiger swallowtail has a similar line, but it is broken into spots. Unlike the eastern tiger swallowtail, females are rarely black. The major caterpillar food plants of this northern butterfly are birches and aspens. Another swallowtail found in the park is the black swallowtail (*P. polyxenes*). It is black with yellow markings; the larvae feed on members of the parsley family.

CABBAGE WHITE
Pieris rapae
White and Sulphur family (Pieridae)
Quick ID: White to yellowish-white; forewing with black tip. Females have one black spot on the wings; males have two black spots.

Wingspan: 1.2–1.7 inches   Flight season: March–November

Thriving in most of North America, the cabbage white butterfly nectars on a wide variety of plants, including mustards, dandelions, clovers, asters, and mints. Native to Asia, Europe, and North Africa, this butterfly was introduced to the United States in the 1800s. The caterpillars of the cabbage white butterfly cause significant crop damage and are considered an agricultural pest.

PINK-EDGED SULPHUR
Colias interior
White and Sulphur family (Pieridae)
Quick ID: Wings yellow with pink edges bordered with black margins and single central spot

Wingspan: 1.5–2.6 inches
Flight season: June–August

In 2023 the pink-edged sulphur was named the official butterfly of the state of Maine thanks to fifth graders from Old Orchard Beach. These nature-loving youngsters wrote a letter to the state representative asking why Maine didn't have a state butterfly. The importance of this pollinator to Maine blueberries crowned the pink-edged sulphur as the state's star butterfly. Widespread in the

Orange sulphur

Northeast and Canada, the pink-edged sulfur can be commonly seen in Maine, where the female lays its eggs on abundant blueberry plants. Adults prefer nectaring on bristly sarsaparilla and orange hawkweed. The similar clouded sulphur (*C. philodice*) has a double ring around a silvery spot on the hind wing and dark spots on the underside of the hind wing. The orange sulphur (*C. eurytheme*) has similar dark spots on the underside of the wings but has an orange patch on the forewing.

AMERICAN COPPER
Lycaena phlaeas
Gossamer-wing family (Lycaenidae)
Quick ID: Upper wing orange-red with black spots; hind wing gray with orange-red outer margin; underside gray with orange zigzag on hind wing

Wingspan: 0.9–1.4 inches   Flight season: June–September

The American copper has an eye-catching fiery orange pattern, making it a treat for butterfly watchers. This small to medium-sized butterfly tends to fly about 1 to 2 feet above the ground, aggressively defending its territory from other butterflies as well as other insects. Found in meadows, fields, and roadsides, they nectar on a variety of flowers. Docks and sheep sorrel are the larvae's food plants. Look for these and other butterflies at Thompson Island Picnic Area.

BOG COPPER
Lycaena epixanthe
Gossamer-wing family (Lycaenidae)
Quick ID: Upper wing of male brownish with purplish iridescence; female similar to coloration of male but duller gray-brown; hindwing with tiny black spots, red zigzag border on outer margin

Wingspan: 0.9–1 inch   Flight season: June–August

As its name suggests, the bog copper is found in acidic bogs in the Northeast. Males of this small butterfly have intense purple upper wings, but the females are dull brown. The adults nectar on cranberry flowers. The host plant for the caterpillars are cranberries, but they may not be found where pesticides have been applied. Many butterflies including the bog copper are dependent on sensitive habitats such as bogs, which are often drained for commercial uses; conservation of these habitats is vital for this small butterfly.

EASTERN PINE ELFIN
Callophrys niphon
Gossamer-wing family (Lycaenidae)
Quick ID: Dark brown with grayish bands
and black crescents

Wingspan: 0.9–1.2 inches
Flight season: March–June

Striped hairstreak

A small butterfly, the eastern pine elfin has distinct gray and black markings on a brown background. Eastern pine elfins lay their eggs on white pine and other pines. When the caterpillars hatch, they feed on the needles. During the cold winter months, they hibernate in a chrysalid, the adults emerging in the spring. The males perch high on the treetops of pines, searching for females. You may see the adults nectaring on the flowers of blueberries, milkweeds, and clovers. Widespread in the East, this butterfly ranges from Nova Scotia to Florida. The striped hairstreak (*Satyrium liparops*) is a similar small brown butterfly, but the hindwings have two tails that mimic antennae to trick a predator into biting a piece of the wing rather than the head. The underside has white stripes, and near the tails are orange crescents bordering blue spots. The larvae feed on blueberry, cherry, and other woody plants, especially those in the Rose family.

SILVERY BLUE
Glaucopsyche
lygdamus
Gossamer-wing family
(Lycaenidae)
Quick ID: Underside
grayish white with black
spots ringed in white
and orange markings;
top of male's wings
blue with dark border;
top of female's wings
brownish with orange
band

Spring azure

Northern azure

Wingspan: 0.9–1.25 inches
Flight season: March–June

Dainty silvery blues flit about, nectaring at asters
in open meadows, revealing the flashes of bright
blue on their upper wings. With patience you can
sometimes see them sunning themselves with
wings open, revealing the dazzling blue coloration.
The underside of their wings is grayish white with
distinguishing markings. Several other small blue
butterflies can be seen in Maine, including the
spring azure (*Celastrina ladon*), summer azure (*C.
neglecta*), northern azure (*C. lucia*), and eastern
tailed blue (*Cupido comyntas*).

Eastern tailed blue

107

Great spangled fritillary

ATLANTIS FRITILLARY
Speyeria atlantis
Brushfoot family (Nymphalidae)
Quick ID: Upper side orangish brown, darker in front with black outer margins; underside with silvery spots

Wingspan: 2–2.75 inches   Flight season: June–September

The orange-and-black color of fritillaries looks similar to the coloration of the better-known monarch butterfly, but fritillaries have a more checked pattern on their wings. The word "fritillary" comes from the Latin *fritillus*, which means "chessboard." Fritillaries are divided into two main categories based on size. Along with the Atlantis fritillary, other large, or greater, fritillaries found in the park include the great spangled fritillary (*S. cybele*) and Aphrodite fritillary (*S. aphrodite*). The smaller silver-bordered fritillary (*Boloria selene*) is one of the lesser fritillaries and is found in bogs and wet meadows. A recent study showed that Atlantis fritillary populations, which prefer cool habitats, have seen a decline in nearby Massachusetts in response to climate change. Fritillary caterpillars feed on violets.

Aphrodite fritillary

Silver-bordered fritillary

NORTHERN CRESCENT
Phyciodes cocyta
Brushfoot family (Nymphalidae)
Quick ID: Orange with dark borders and markings; underside orange with tan patch. Males have antennae tipped with orange; females have darker-tipped antennae.

Wingspan: 1.25–1.87 inches
Flight season: June–July

This small northern butterfly is very similar to the pearl crescent, but pearl crescents have black antennae tips as opposed to the orange tips of the male northern crescent. Northern crescents have been recently separated from pearl crescents (*P. tharos*), and there is still some uncertainty about whether they are actually a separate species. The range of northern crescents is more northern than that of the pearl crescent. Females lay their eggs on the underside of asters, which are the host plant for caterpillars. Crescents get their common name from the crescent-shaped spot on their hind wing.

Pearl crescent

109

HARRIS' CHECKERSPOT
Chlosyne harrisii
Brushfoot family (Nymphalidae)
Quick ID: Upper side orange with black markings with black margin; underside reddish orange with white and black patterns

Wingspan: 1.4–2 inches
Flight season: June–July

Resembling northern crescents, Harris' checkerspot butterflies have similar orange and black markings, but they are even more distinct. Checkerspot butterfly species are abundant in the western states, but only a handful are found in the East. Baltimore checkerspot (*Euphydryas phaeton*) and silvery checkerspot (*Chlosyne nycteis*) are the only other checkerspots that can potentially be found in Maine. Harris' checkerspot is an uncommon northern species that ranges from the Northeast into the Upper Midwest states and Canada. Look for this striking butterfly in wet meadows and boggy areas. The host plant for the caterpillar is the flat-topped white aster (*Aster umbellatus*).

Baltimore checkerspot

MOURNING CLOAK
Nymphalis antiopa
Brushfoot family (Nymphalidae)

Quick ID: Ragged brownish-maroon upper side bordered with a broad yellow band and blue spots; underside dark brown with dark striations

Wingspan: 2.5–4 inches   Flight season: June–July

Gracefully gliding through the crisp spring air, the mourning cloak is a beautiful and much appreciated harbinger of spring. A broad irregular yellow border and a row of bright blue spots complement the velvety purplish-brown wings of this butterfly. They overwinter in sheltered crevices and may come out of hibernation on warm winter days to feed on running sap and decaying matter.

AMERICAN LADY
Vanessa virginiensis
Brushfoot family (Nymphalidae)
Quick ID: Upper parts orange
with dark markings and small
white spots near front edge; two
eyespots on underside of hind wing

Wingspan: 1.75–2.4 inches
Flight season: April–October

A very common and pretty butterfly,
the American lady is orange with
dark markings and two "eyespots"
on the underside of the hind wing.
The very similar painted lady (*V.
cardui*) has four small eyespots
on the underside of the hind

wing. With an erratic flight these butterflies nectar at a variety of flowers, including milkweeds, asters, goldenrod, and sunflowers. Caterpillar host plants include pussytoes and burdock.

WHITE ADMIRAL
Limenitis arthemis
Brushfoot family (Nymphalidae)
Quick ID: Upper wings black with broad white bands and row of blue dashes with red dots; underwings reddish brown with white bands

Wingspan: 2.3–3.9 inches   Flight season: June–September

The trickster of the butterfly world, the white admiral has two totally different forms that historically placed it in two separate species. In the North, the white admiral is widespread and commonly seen along forest edges, trails, and streams. In the South, the red-spotted purple form is a commonly seen butterfly. This form lacks the broad white bands of the white admiral. Where the two forms overlap, the intergrade results are highly variable in color. The host plants for caterpillars are willows, aspen, and birch.

MONARCH
Danaus plexippus
Brushfoot family (Nymphalidae)
Quick ID: Orange with black veins, white spots on black wing borders

Wingspan: 3.5–4.5 inches   Flight season: April–October

One of the most well-known and beloved of all members of the insect world, the monarch easily lives up to its celebrity status. The yellow and black–striped caterpillars feed on plants in the milkweed family, ingesting toxins that render them distasteful to predators. Carrying these toxins into adulthood, the orange and black coloration warning is recognized by predators and confers parallel protection to other similarly colored butterflies such as the viceroy (*Limenitis archippus*). In fall, monarchs migrate by the thousands to Mexico, where they overwinter before their offspring make the long journey back. Look for monarchs at many of the wonderful public gardens on Mount Desert Island, including Asticou Azalea Garden, Abby Aldrich Rockefeller Garden, Thuya Garden, Charlotte Rhoades Park and Butterfly Garden, and Wild Gardens of Acadia. Consider including a visit to the Coastal Maine Botanical Gardens in Boothbay, where you can visit their butterfly house for a close look at many butterfly species native to Maine.

EYED BROWN
Satyrodes eurydice
Brushfoot family (Nymphalidae)
Quick ID: Tannish brown with variable dark eyespots near wing margins; dark zigzag line on underside of hind wing

Wingspan: 1.5–2.4 inches   Flight season: June–September

Even though it may not be the most stunning butterfly in the field, the eyed brown is commonly seen in moist meadows and open marshes in the park. As it flies weakly over low plants, the distinctive rows of circular eyespots are good identification marks. Sedges are the host plants for the caterpillars. The adults feed on tree sap, bird droppings, and flower nectar. The similar but larger northern pearly-eye (*Enodia anthedon*) is found in more-wooded areas and often sits on tree trunks with its head pointing down. It is attracted to

Little wood satyr

rotting fruit. The little wood satyr (*Megisto cymela*), with its bouncy flight along woodland edges, is easily recognized, even if you don't see the two large eyespots on each wing. The harvester (*Feniseca tarquinius*) has orangish-brown spots encircled with white.

COMMON RINGLET
Coenonympha tullia
Brushfoot family (Nymphalidae)
Quick ID: Forewing underside
orange-brown with one eyespot;
hind wing darker yellowish brown
with irregular white band

Wingspan: 1.3–1.5 inches
Flight season: May–July

The common ringlet is widespread
but often overlooked, as its small
size and soft colors make it
inconspicuous. It is also known as
ochre ringlet due to the pale orange-
brown coloration of the upper wings.
It frequently nectars on low flowers

Common wood-nymph

in moist meadows. The larger, darker common wood-nymph (*Cercyonis pegala*) is found along woodland
edges and open brushy meadows.

ARCTIC SKIPPER
Carterocephalus palaemon
Skipper family (Hesperiidae)

Quick ID: Upper side black with square orange spots; underside yellowish brown with large white spots

Wingspan: 1–1.25 inches   Flight season: May–July

One of the few boreal butterfly species in Maine, the arctic skipper is found in northern North America and in subarctic habitats. Skippers are a subset of butterflies that have larger heads and bodies, smaller wings, and hooked antennae. Their rapid, skipping flight pattern resembles that of moths. Most skippers are various shades of brown with small inconspicuous markings, making many members of this family a challenge to identify. Fortunately, the markings on a few skippers such as the arctic skipper distinguish them from their counterparts. This northern beauty is brownish black with squarish orange spots; the males perch on low vegetation looking for potential mates. Found in moist meadows and boggy areas, the adults will nectar at wild irises and other flowers; the caterpillars feed on grasses. Other skippers that can be found in Acadia include the long dash (*Polites mystic*), common Hobomok skipper (*Poanes hobomok*), and local pepper and salt skipper (*Amblyscirtes hegon*).

ng dash

Common Hobomok skipper

Pepper and salt skipper

LUNA MOTH
Actias luna
Saturniid Moth family (Saturniidae)
Quick ID: Very large lime-green; long
twisted tails; elliptical eyespots

Wingspan: 3.0–4.1 inches
Flight season: May–July

Unmistakable even at night, the very large
luna moth is attracted to lights around
buildings and parking lots. They rest during
the day on trees with their wings flattened.
The long, twisted, paddle-shaped tails are
a defense mechanism meant to confuse

the echolocation of bats. After emerging from their cocoons, adults live only about one week. During
this week, they do not eat, and their prime objective is to find a mate. Males are lighter green and have
antennae that fan out like a feather; females are more vivid green and have slender fuzzy antennae. The
caterpillars feed on birch, beech, and willows as well as other plants. The species name is from Luna,
Roman goddess of the moon.

SPRUCE BUDWORM MOTH
Choristoneura fumiferana
Leafroller Moth family (Tortricidae)
Quick ID: Gray with rust; wings with silvery patches

Wingspan: 0.9–1.2 inches
Flight season: July–August

The spruce budworm is a native species of moth that is considered one of the most destructive insects of forest trees in the North. The caterpillars feed on spruce and fir needles and buds. Outbreaks of spruce budworm have occurred periodically every thirty to sixty years for thousands of years in northern New England and Canada.

Brown hooded owlet caterpillar

Birds such as evening grosbeaks take advantage of the plentiful food supply, increasing the survival of young birds, some of which may head south. Predators of the moths include birds and other insects, including dragonflies. Another moth found in Acadia is the brown hooded owlet (*Cucullia convexipennis*). The lightly striped tannish-brown adults are nondescript, with a projection over their head that resembles a hood. The large poisonous caterpillars, however, are stunningly marked with warning coloration of broad yellow side stripes and an orangish-red stripe down the back. The caterpillars feed on asters and goldenrods.

BROWNTAIL MOTH
Euproctis chrysorrhoea
Erebid Moth family (Erebidae)

Quick ID: Adults white with brown tail; 1.5-inch caterpillars brown with broken white strip and tufts along the sides, two reddish-orange dots on the tail end

Wingspan: 1.4–1.6 inches
Flight season: July–August

Browntail moth caterpillars are well known to Mainers as a caterpillar to be avoided. These non-native invasive moths were accidentally introduced into Massachusetts from Europe in the late 1800s, and browntail moths are now found

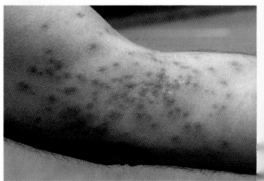

Skin rash from browntail moth hairs

in all New England states and Canada. From April through June, caterpillars emerge from their winter web home and feed on the leaves of host trees including oak, birch, fruit trees, roses, and other hardwoods. The adult moths are not considered dangerous, but the caterpillars are covered in toxic barbed hairs that easily break off, causing health problems for people. The barbed hairs can cause severe rashes that itch and burn, resembling a rash from poison ivy. The hairs can also become airborne and cause significant respiratory problems. The microscopic hairs can remain toxic in the environment for one to three years. Mainers have learned tactics to avoid the stinging hairs, including avoiding hanging laundry outside during spring and summer, wearing masks and protective clothing when doing yardwork, and trimming the webs from branches in fall.

HUMMINGBIRD CLEARWING MOTH
Hemaris thysbe
Sphinx Moth family (Sphingidae)
Quick ID: Golden-olive back; yellow belly; abdomen dark burgundy; wings mostly clear with dark reddish borders

Total length: 1–1.2 inches   Flight season: March–October

Not much larger than a bee, the hummingbird clearwing moth is aptly named, as its appearance and behavior often cause it to be mistaken for a tiny hummingbird. Active during the day, they can be seen nectaring at tubular flowers such as honeysuckles, thistles, and bee balm. The moths have a long, coiled mouthpart called a proboscis that it uncoils to dip into a flower to sip nectar.

BLACKLEGGED TICK

Ixodes scapularis

Hard Tick family (Ixodidae)

Quick ID: Tiny, flat, dark brown body; red abdomen on females; 8 legs as adult, 6 legs as nymph

Length: 0.04–0.12 inch

Commonly known as deer ticks from their association with white-tailed deer, blacklegged ticks are widespread in the eastern United States and Canada. Found throughout Maine, these tiny arachnids have become infamous as vectors of Lyme disease, which is caused by a spiral-shaped bacterium (*Borrelia burgdorferi*) found in infected deer ticks. The most common symptoms are a characteristic bull's-eye rash called erythema migrans that occurs from three to thirty days after exposure in 70 to 80 percent of cases. Fever, headache, and fatigue are possible in the first few weeks. Lyme disease can be treated with antibiotics, but left untreated it can lead to arthritis and other conditions. Ticks are found throughout Acadia, especially in areas with deciduous forests. Make sure to protect yourself from tick bites by applying insect repellent, tucking your pants into your socks, wearing light-colored clothing, and performing a "tick check" after being outdoors. Ticks can be safely removed with a special tick remover spoon or fine-point tweezers.

TRICOLORED BUMBLEBEE
Bombus ternarius
Bee family (Apidae)

Quick ID: Plump body covered in hairs; black head; several yellow abdominal segments; 2 middle abdominal segments orange, last segment black or with yellow on the sides

Length: 0.31–0.51 inch

Bumblebees have long tongues to reach into flowers as well as specialized pollen baskets on their hind legs. Bumblebees also dislodge pollen by vibrating their flight muscles, an action called buzz pollination. Bumblebees are not typically aggressive unless provoked. With their bright orange abdominal segments, tricolored bumblebees are very

Yellow-banded bumblebee

colorful. Tricolored bumblebees live in underground colonies of between 50 and 500 individuals. They are valuable pollinators of many plants, including many wild plants such as blueberries. Bumblebees and other pollinators are facing issues such as habitat loss, pesticides, and introduced diseases and other insects. Yellow-banded bumblebees (*B. terricola*) have bands of yellow on a black body. Native to the northern United States and southern Canada, they have greatly declined in numbers due to urban development, climate change, and parasite and fungal infections. Similar to the tricolored bumblebee, the rusty-patched bumble bee (*B. affinis*) has a spot of orange on its back and is critically endangered.

123

BLACKFLY
Simulium sp.
Blackfly family (Simuliidae)
Quick ID: Small, black or grayish with shiny thorax and humpbacked shape; small head with large round eyes; short legs; very short antennae; clear wings

Length: 0.04–0.23 inch

Visitors to Acadia may not be familiar with the tiny black flies that have a nasty bite. About forty species of blackflies can be found in Maine, but of these only four or five species feed on people. Males feed on nectar, and it is only the females that bite. All blackflies have serrated jaws to cut the skin, and their saliva contains an anticoagulant that partially numbs the site while

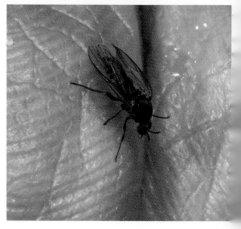

the fly feeds on the blood meal. They typically fly only during the day and tend to bite thinner skin such as at hairline, neck, ears, arms, or ankles. They are attracted to dark colors such as black or navy blue, so wearing white or pale colors can help. The bites can cause itching, swelling, and inflammation. Blackflies require clean, running water in which to breed and are highly sensitive to polluted water.

HEMLOCK WOOLLY ADELGID
Adelges tsugae
Adelgid family (Adelgidae)
Quick ID: Tiny reddish-purple, aphid-like insect; covered by white waxy secretion

Length: 0.03 inch

Introduced from East Asia, the hemlock woolly adelgid is a tiny aphid-like insect that has decimated large stands of stately eastern hemlock trees. An adult adelgid is smaller than the period at the end of a sentence, but it damages hemlock trees by sucking sap from twigs. The needles dry out and fall off, followed by complete destruction of the branches. Trees often die within four years of infestation. This invasive insect was first discovered in Acadia National Park in 2022. The white, woolly egg sacs are found under the needles. Park biologists are taking measures to save the regal hemlock trees in the park. Another small insect that creates white cottony filaments, alder psyllids (*Psylla* sp.) are sapsucking insects on alders. The nymphs are covered in fluffy, waxy secretions that may protect the insect from predators.

Alder psyllid

Alder psyllid tended by ants

ROBBER FLY BUMBLEBEE MIMIC
Laphria posticata
Robber Fly family (Asilidae)
Quick ID: Yellow bristles on face; yellow bristles on back; black bristles on end; short, straight, stubby antennae; one pair of wings

Length: 0.4–1.1 inches

A master of mimicry, the robber fly bumblebee mimic is a fly that looks like a common bumblebee. Lying in wait on a leaf, a robber fly grabs an unsuspecting victim then uses its daggerlike proboscis to inject venom to paralyze its victim. It also injects powerful enzymes that turn the insides of the victim into a nutritious "soup" for the robber fly to suck up through its straw-like proboscis. Also called assassin flies, their prey includes wasps, bees, butterflies, and beetles. The robber fly bumblebee mimic prefers to rest on white pine logs and stumps. Bees have two pairs of wings and jointed antennae, while flies have only one pair of wings and short, straight antennae. Robber flies lack stingers, but if handled they can deliver a painful "bite" with their sharp proboscis.

TRANVERSE BANDED FLOWER FLY
Eristalis transversa
Hover Fly family (Syrphidae)
Quick ID: Gray on front half of body and black on rear half, with black and bright yellow stripes and markings; 2 wings; 2 large brown eyes

Length: 0.35–0.43 inch

The transverse banded flower fly is a common type of hover fly. Also called drone flies or flower flies, these harmless flies so closely resemble bees or wasps that any predator would think twice before trying to snatch one up. This form of mimicry, called Batesian mimicry, is where a harmless species has evolved to imitate the warning coloration of a dangerous species to fool predators. Hover flies are so named for their ability to hover over a flower before dropping down to enjoy the sweet nectar and protein-rich pollen. Another fly that resembles a bumblebee is the orange legged drone fly (*Eristalis flavipes*). The middle and back legs are orangish, leading to its common name.

Orange legged drone fly

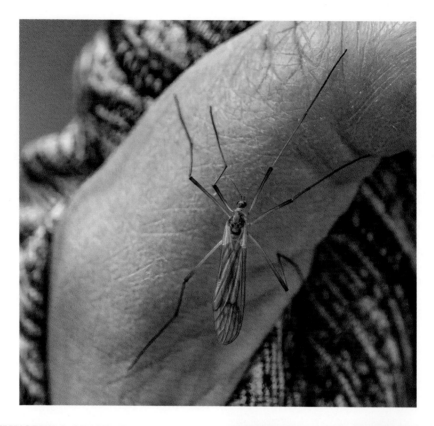

LIMNOPHILA CRANE FLY
Limnophila sp.
Limnophila Crane Fly family (Limoniidae)
Quick ID: Looks like a giant mosquito with elongated body; long slender legs; long, narrow, patterned wings held along the back of the body

Length: 0.5–2 inches

Sure to command attention with its needlelike body and long legs, the crane fly looks like a giant mosquito. Totally harmless, crane flies are not mosquitoes at all, and they do not bite or sting. Their long stilt-like legs are similar to those of tall birds called cranes, hence the common name. Important members of the food chain, they are typically found near wet areas, where they are nabbed by birds, fish, frogs, and other insects. Limoniidae is the largest of four crane fly families, with over 10,000 species. Limnophila crane flies hold their wings along the back of the body, while

Yellow-bellied sapsucker with crane flies

other crane flies usually hold them out at right angles. To add a nutritious sweet boost, yellow-bellied sapsuckers dip captured crane flies in sap before carrying them off to feed to their young.

MOSQUITO
Aedes sp.
Mosquito family (Culicidae)

Quick ID: Two wings; 6 spindly legs; long feathery antennae; proboscis; 2 large compound eyes

Length: 0.11–0.24 inch

Spanish for "little fly," mosquitos are small flies that feed on the blood of various hosts, and there are 3,700 species of them. The all-too-familiar itchy rash is caused by the mosquito's saliva, which is transferred when it bites. Only the female requires a protein-rich blood meal, after which she lays her eggs then repeats the process. Males feed on nectar, living only about five to seven days. Mosquitoes in the genus *Aedes* have characteristic black and white markings on their legs and body. Thirty-four species of mosquitoes have been found in Maine. They use their antennae to detect carbon dioxide that a person breathes out.

CRESTED PYGMY GRASSHOPPER
Nomotettix cristatus
Pygmy Grasshopper family (Tetrigidae)

Quick ID: Speckled brownish gray; elongated first body section (pronotum)

Length: 0.24–0.43 inch

Found in the eastern United States and Canada, the crested pygmy grasshopper prefers dry locations with rocks and lichens such as those found on Cadillac Mountain. Here the grasshopper is camouflaged against the lichen-covered granite, helping it avoid predation. It is also known as rock lichen pygmy grasshopper or crested grouse locust.

GOLDENROD CRAB SPIDER
Misumena vatia
Crab Spider family (Thomisidae)
Quick ID: Flattened body with crablike legs; male darker reddish brown, whitish body with brownish marks, first two pairs of legs reddish brown, last two pairs of legs yellowish; female white to yellow with red band on sides, pale legs

Length: 0.12–0.35 inch

Resembling tiny crabs, these spiders sit motionless on flowers waiting for passing prey insects such as bees, wasps, or flies. One of the few spider species capable of changing colors, after several days they gradually assume the color of their surrounding flower heads. When a suitable insect is within range, the spider grasps it quickly with its front legs and injects its victim with venom to immobilize it. In vampire fashion, the spider then sucks the bodily fluids out.

EBONY JEWELWING
Calopteryx maculata
Broad-winged Damselfly
family (Calopterygidae)
Quick ID: Male has metallic blue-green body; black wings. Female is dull brown; smoky wings with white spots near the tips.

Length: 1.5–2.2 inches

Damselflies can easily be mistaken for the closely related dragonflies, but there are some characteristics that help separate the two. The wings of damselflies are narrow, and at

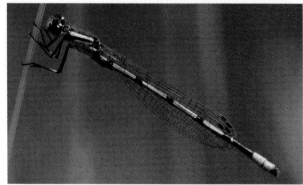

Hagen's bluet

rest damselflies typically hold their wings close to their bodies; dragonflies have broad rounded wings that they hold open. Also, damselflies have small eyes that are separated, while dragonflies have very large eyes that cover most of their head. Ebony jewelwings are damselflies with a brilliant metallic green body that often looks blue in the sunlight. Hagen's bluet (*Enallagma hageni*) is another striking damselfly with blue and black stripes on the body. The female Hagen's bluet has light brown to bluish or green colors with a black back.

TWELVE-SPOTTED SKIMMER
Libellula pulchella
Skimmer family (Libellulidae)
Quick ID: Males have bluish-white body; 12 brown and 8 white wings spots. Females are brownish with yellow side stripe and lack the white wing spots.

Length: 1.9–2.1 inches

The abundant wetlands, ponds, and streams in Acadia are perfect habitat for dragonflies. Dragonflies have existed for more than 300 million years, and some prehistoric species boasted a 2.5-foot wingspan. Even though today's dragonflies are much smaller, they are extremely productive predators with a 97 percent success capture rate for flies, mosquitoes, bees, and other insects. With more than 1,000 species worldwide, skimmers are the largest family of dragonflies. Some have imaginative common names, such as

Four-spotted skimmer

Common whitetail

Chalk fronted corporal

White corporal

meadowhawks, pondhawks, gliders, dashers, and saddlebags. The twelve-spotted skimmer is found in all forty-eight of the contiguous United States and into southern Canada. Males have white and black spots on their wings; females lack the white spots.

Eastern pondhawk

Racket tailed emerald

Dot tailed whiteface

Crimson ringed whiteface

Springtime darner

Green darner

SUGAR KELP
Saccharina latissima
Kelp family (Laminariaceae)
Quick ID: Long golden-brown blade; long, narrow undivided, short thin stem; wavy edge

Length: To 16 feet

Sugar kelp is a brown alga found in the North Atlantic Ocean and along the coast of North America north of Massachusetts. There are over 250 species of seaweed in the Gulf of Maine. Sugar kelp is also known as sea belt and devil's apron, as the long blade can grow up to 16 feet long and 8 inches wide. Packed with vitamins and minerals, kelp is being used by inventive chefs to create inspired umami-rich dishes that have been shown to reduce inflammation and help prevent weight gain.

BLADDER WRACK
Fucus vesiculosus
Brown Algae family (Fucaceae)
Quick ID: Olive-brown 1-inch-wide flat, strap-like fronds with paired, round air bladders within the blade; midrib along frond; often forms large mats on rocks in the tidal zone

Length: To 59 inches

Seaweeds are marine algae, most of which are attached by anchoring structures called holdfasts. They are divided into three main categories according to general color: brown, green, and red algae. Worldwide there are over 9,000 species of seaweed, some of which are considered delicacies; others are used in cosmetics or as fertilizers. Bladder wrack, or rockweed, is one of the common seaweeds in the waters around the coast of Acadia. The most notable feature is the round air bladders, which help it float toward available sunlight. According to the National Institutes of Health, seaweed is the best source of iodine, a necessary ingredient to prevent hypothyroidism and goiter. Another common seaweed,

Knotted wrack

which can reach a length of 78 inches, knotted wrack (*Ascophyllum nodosum*) has thin branching fronds with football-shaped air bladders. Often growing with knotted wrack, twisted rockweed (*F. spiralis*) has twisted blades and terminal, slightly ridged or winged receptacles.

Close-up of knotted wrack

Knotted wrack bordered by bladder wrack

135

IRISH MOSS
Chondrus crispus
Red Algae family (Gigartinaceae)
Quick ID: Dark red, slimy broad branches

Length: To 7.8 inches

Irish moss is a dark red parsley-like seaweed that grows attached to rocks. A species of red algae, it has mucusy strands made of carrageenan. Carrageenan is a polysaccharide that forms a gel when cooked, and since the fifteenth century has been widely used in food preparation as a thickener. In recent years, carrageenans have been used in the health-care field to cover wounds, in tissue engineering, and delivering drugs including extended-release tablets.

COMMON PERIWINKLE
Littorina littorea
Sea Snail family (Littorinidae)
Quick ID: Grayish to gray-brown, often with dark spiral bands; slightly flattened spiral shell with white outer lip, brown inside shell

Length: 0.6–1.5 inches

Common periwinkles, or winkles, are sea snails that dine on algae that grows on rocks and seaweeds. A larger, heavier sea snail, the dog whelk (*Thais lapillus*) has a more pointed spiral shell with a groove at the opening; shell may be banded with a variety of colors, including creamy brown or yellowish orange. Whelks are carnivorous and use a modified tooth, called a radula, to bore holes in the shells of prey; they then insert enzymes to break down the prey's body. Periwinkles and whelks are traditionally found on local dinner plates. They are either steamed, boiled, or pickled.

BLUE MUSSEL
Mytilus edulis
True Mussel family (Mytilidae)
Quick ID: Two dark glossy bluish-black
elongated curved shells joined by a hinge;
concentric lines from hinge

Length: 1–4 inches

Blue mussels are native to coastal Maine
and are commonly seen in tide pools. They
attach to rocks and other structures by
threadlike structures called byssal threads.
The word "byssal" is derived from the
Latin *byssus* ("sea silk"). Mussels are filter

feeders, extracting tiny plants and animals from the water. In Maine, blue mussels are harvested using
aquaculture techniques in which mussels attach to ropes and are allowed to grow. Mussels are regularly
served as a delicious local food from the sea. The byssal threads are commonly referred to as the "beard"
of the mussel.

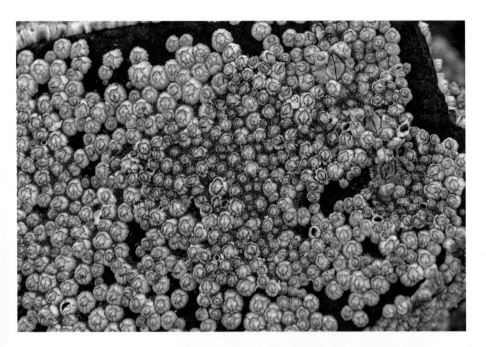

ACORN BARNACLE
Semibalanus balanoides
Barnacle family (Balanidae)
Quick ID: Six grayish-white wall plates; feathery appendages

Length: 1–2.5 inches

Acorn barnacles, or common rock barnacles, live their lives attached to rocks and other solid structures such as piers. Found in cold waters of the Northeast, acorn barnacles have six grayish-white wall plates that surround the mouth. When covered with water, they extend

feathery structures called cirri to filter tiny floating organisms, or zooplankton, from the ocean water. Barnacles are aware of light and will retreat into their shells when threatened. Sea stars prey on barnacles.

AMERICAN LOBSTER
Homarus americanus
Clawed Lobster family
(Nephropidae)
Quick ID: Rusty brownish
green; large bodied with spiny
exoskeleton; 10 legs with the front
2 as large claws

Length: 1–3.5 feet   Weight:
0.5–44 pounds

Like peanut butter and jelly,
Maine and lobsters just naturally
go together. Maine is the largest
lobster-producing state in the
country, and travelers from around

the world come to Maine to try their first lobster dinner. So iconic to Maine, in 2016 the lobster was
named the official state crustacean. The first pair of legs on the lobster are modified into two large claws.
The largest claw has rounded nubs and is used for crushing prey; the smaller claw has sharp inner edges
and is used to help subdue and dismantle prey. Lobsters were so common and ungainly that early English
colonists used them as fertilizer and gave them to the poor. Lobsters are generally brownish green and only
turn red after cooking as pigments in the shell break down. Maine lobsters are the largest crustaceans and
can reach a record weight of 44 pounds, but the average adult is about 1 pound. Research shows that the
Gulf of Maine is warming faster than most of the world's oceans; this will eventually affect the lobster
population.

ACADIAN HERMIT CRAB
Pagurus acadianus
Hermit Crab family (Paguridae)
Quick ID: Reddish-brown, long spirally curved abdomen; 5 pair of legs with the first pair as enlarged claws, one larger than the other

Length: 1–3 inches

Hermit crabs are small crustaceans, with more than 800 species worldwide. They get their name because they go from shell home to shell home, never staying in the same shell. Just like children that grow out of their shoes, growing hermit crabs seek out larger shells to live in, such as discarded shells of sea snails. Unlike true crabs, hermit crabs have a soft tail with a hard exoskeleton only on the front part of their body.

GREEN CRAB
Carcinus maenas
Swimming Crab family (Portunidae)
Quick ID: Dark green to yellowish; back shell (carapace) wider in front than the back; 3 rounded lobes between the eyes; carapace with 5 marginal teeth; narrow claws with last pair of legs slightly flattened

Length: 1–3 inches

This small crab has five pointed spines on each side of the shell, or carapace. Even though it is called a green crab, the color may vary from green to yellowish. In the intertidal zone, voracious green crabs dine on

Jonah crab

clams, oysters, mussels, and other delicacies. Unfortunately, this crab is not native to Maine and is causing havoc with these native species. Rising ocean temperatures have favored this crab, and numbers have soared. Since the early 1900s, this European crab species has become very destructive to native species, and efforts are underway to reduce populations, including encouraging restaurants to offer them on their menus. Green crabs are in direct competition for food with native crab species. Native species such as the Jonah crab (*Cancer borealis*) have smooth carapaces with greater than five teeth per side. The Jonah crab has a rounded, lightly spotted carapace with rough edges and robust claws with dark tips.

GREEN SEA URCHIN
Strongylocentrotus droebachiensis
Sea Urchin family
(Strongylocentrotidae)
Quick ID: Greenish, round slightly flattened shell, called a test, made of interlocking plates with long thin spines; tiny claws on surface called pedicellaria between the spines

Length: 0.02–3.15 inches

Mouth

Along with sea stars, sea cucumbers, and sand dollars, sea urchins are echinoderms and are recognized by their radial symmetry. Echinoderm means "hedgehog skin," in reference to the spiny shell. Resembling a pincushion full of needles, these small balls of spines use these "needles" for defense and locomotion. On the underside of their body, their five jaws with complex toothlike structures are arranged in a circular pattern called Aristotle's lantern, which they use to scrape algae off rocks. The Greek philosopher Aristotle described the structure like a "horn lantern," which is a five-sided lantern made of thin pieces of horn. Although the spines of some species of sea urchins are venomous, those of the green sea urchin are not.

If you accidentally step on one, however, the spines can break off in the skin, causing pain, swelling, and infection.

NORTHERN SEA STAR
Asterias rubens
Sea Star family (Asteriidae)
Quick ID: Color varies from orange to brownish or violet; radially symmetrical with 5 spiny arms; pale yellow spot in center

Length: 4–11.5 inches

The northern or common sea star is a favorite of tide pool adventurers. Sea stars have an excellent sense of smell and detect prey such as mussels, one

Suction cups

of their favorite foods. Using its strong tube feet, the sea star opens the mussel enough to insert a fold of its stomach, which secretes powerful enzymes to liquefy the mussel into a "soup." Besides the northern sea star, a very similar relative in the Gulf of Maine, Forbes sea star (*A. forbesi*) has a darker orange center spot. Search for these and other marine animals in tide pools, but please do not pull sea stars from where they are attached; it can damage their arms.

WHITE PINE
Pinus strobus
Pine family (Pinaceae)

Quick ID: Tall evergreen; 3- to 5-inch needles in bundles of 5; bark with deep furrows; 4- to 8-inch cones, slender and tapered toward the end, often dotted with sap

Height: 80–110 feet

More than 80 percent of Maine is covered with forests, and the high quality of white pine as lumber has played an important role in the economy of the state. Early colonists used white pines as ship masts, and pine resin was used to waterproof baskets and wooden pails. So important is the tree to the state that in 1893 the white pine was declared the official floral emblem of Maine and in 1945 was named the official state tree. The tree appears on the state flag, state seal, and the Maine quarter. Maine has even been dubbed the "Pine Tree State" in reference to the importance of the white pine. The only pine with five needles bundled together in the East makes this tree easy to identify. Another member of this family, red pine (*P. resinosa*) has needles in bundles of two that break with a distinct crispness when bent. Red pines are under siege by a tiny scale insect called red pine scale (*Matsucoccus matsumurae*), as well as two fungal diseases.

PITCH PINE
Pinus rigida
Pine family (Pinaceae)

Quick ID: Evergreen; 3 twisted coarse, stiff needles per fascicle, 2.5–5 inches long; cones 2–4 inches long with short, stout recurved prickles; bark thick flat plates with deep furrows; needles frequently growing directly out of the tree trunk

Height: 40–60 feet

Pitch pine is not a common pine in Maine, but it can be found in open woodlands and along coastal areas, reaching its northern limit near Mount Desert Island. It is typically found on rock outcrops and ledges and is one of the only pines that is somewhat salt-tolerant. Pitch pine is rated as vulnerable in Maine due to its restricted range and limited populations. To help identify pitch pine, a good clue is to look for twisted needles in bundles of three. The dense wood has been used to build boats and buildings. You can see pitch pine on Dorr and Champlain Mountains and along Wonderland Trail.

Bark

JACK PINE
Pinus banksiana
Pine family (Pinaceae)

Quick ID: Evergreen; 2 straight or slightly twisted needles per fascicle, 0.75–1.5 inches long; cones 1.25–2 inches long with varied shapes and prickle when young, cones pointing forward along the branch; reddish-brown bark thin, flaky

Height: 30–72 feet

Jack pines, also called gray or scrub pines, are trees of the northern climates and in the park can be found growing in rocky or sandy soil in Schoodic Peninsula. Like pitch pine, these

Cone

trees grow in irregular shrubby shapes. The persistent cones are fire dependent (serotinous) to release the seeds and remain closed until opened by intense heat. Previously on the endangered species list, Kirtland's warbler is dependent on Jack pine habitat for breeding in Michigan. Young Jack pines are an alternate host for sweet fern blister rust (*Cronartium comptoniae*), which forms orange cankers on the trunk and galls on the lower branches. Along the coast at Schoodic Point, the trees take on a flattened 1- to 2-foot-tall growth form caused by the extreme coastal wind and cold, which kills the terminal buds.

147

TAMARACK
Larix laricina
Pine family (Pinaceae)
Quick ID: Small, 0.75- to 1.25-inch soft needles in clusters on spur twigs; small cones, 0.37–0.87 inch

Height: 40–80 feet

Tamarack is an eye-catching tree and one of the easiest to identify. Unique among its fellow conifers, tamarack is deciduous, meaning it loses its needles in autumn just like maples, oaks, and birches. Found in wooded swamps and bogs, the ten to twenty short, soft needles are at the ends of warty spur twigs. Also known as American larch, or hackmatack, the name tamarack comes from the Algonquin word *akemantak*, referring to the use of the tough but pliable wood, which was used to make snowshoes. In late fall the needles turn brilliant yellow and then orange before dropping for the winter.

Cones

BALSAM FIR
Abies balsamea
Pine family (Pinaceae)
Quick ID: Steeple-shaped evergreen; flat needles about 1 inch long, whitish beneath, with broad circular base not attached to the twig with a peg-like structure like a spruce; purplish to green upright cones, 1–3 inches long

Height: 40–60 feet

With aromatic foliage, the stately balsam fir is often chosen for Christmas decorations, and for those growing up with these traditions, it is associated with the smell of the holidays. It is the only fir native to the Northeast and is common in the cold conditions found in Maine and Canada. When the cones fall apart in late autumn, they leave behind noticeable upright pegs. The fragrant needles were used to make pillows, and the boughs were used as sleeping mats. The sticky resin, called balsam, was used as a salve for burns, sores, and cuts. The sap was also chewed for colds; it was melted on hot stones, and the fumes were inhaled for headaches. It has also been used as a transparent glue for glasses and to prepare microscope slides.

EASTERN HEMLOCK
Tsuga canadensis
Pine family (Pinaceae)
Quick ID: Pyramidal evergreen; flat single 0.5-inch-long needles with 2 white lines below; 0.75-inch cone; drooping branches

Height: 60–70 feet

With graceful drooping branches, the eastern hemlock is one of the most beautiful members of the pine family. Native to northeastern North America, their short needles are soft, and they have the smallest cones in the family. You can see these tall trees in the park along the Hemlock Path in Sieur de Monts. An aphid-like insect called the hemlock woolly adelgid has had a major impact on the forests of the East. Accidently introduced from Asia in the 1920s, this tiny scale insect has killed most of the old-growth hemlocks in Great Smoky Mountains and Shenandoah National Parks and has now been found in Acadia.

RED SPRUCE
Picea rubens
Pine family (Pinaceae)
Quick ID: Evergreen; narrow conical crown; pointed needles dark yellowish green and 4-sided, 0.5–0.62 inch; downward-hanging cones; reddish bark in scales; twigs and buds hairy

Height: 60–80 feet

Cone of red spruce

Spruce needles are four-sided and join the branch in single points. If rolled between your fingers, the needles feel spiky. Red spruce is the most common spruce in the park. It grows straight and is conical in shape. Red spruce is often used to make guitars and violins. The sap was used to make spruce chewing gum. The closely related black spruce (*P. mariana*) grows in bogs and swamps. Black spruce branches were historically boiled and used to make spruce beer. When crushed, the needles of white spruce (*P. glauca*) have a pungent odor that some people report smells like cat urine, giving rise to the descriptive common names of cat or skunk spruce.

Spruce ID Chart

	Needles	Twigs	Cone	Cone Scale Margin	Habitat
Black Spruce	Blue-green, dull with waxy bloom	Hairy, glandular	Round, 0.5–1.5 inches; cones remain on the tree for many years	Ragged	Bogs/wetlands
Red Spruce	Yellow-green, very shiny	Hairy	Round to elongate, 1.25–2 inches; most cones fall off the tree each year	Smooth or slightly toothed	Inland and coastal forests
White Spruce	Blue-green to dark green, dull with waxy bloom, smell of cat urine	Smooth	Elongate, 2 inches; most cones fall off the tree each year	Smooth	Maritime, spruce-fir forests, old fields

Cone of black spruce

Black spruce

Cone of white spruce

White spruce

NORTHERN WHITE CEDAR
Thuja occidentalis
Cypress family (Cupressaceae)
Quick ID: Evergreen; flat scale-like yellowish-green leaves; tapered trunk twisted and usually divided; reddish-brown to gray bark in fibrous, shreddy strips; small yellowish-brown 0.37-inch cones in clusters at ends of branches

Height: 40–50 feet

Northern white cedar is native to the northeastern United States and Canada to the Great Lakes. This small to medium tree grows slowly and can live more than 400 years if not damaged by fire. The flattened leaves are arranged like graceful feathery fans, and more than one hundred cultivars have been produced for home gardens, using the name arborvitae, which means "tree of life." The sap, bark, and twigs have been used medicinally, and a tea using the twigs and bark was used to prevent scurvy, a disease caused by a vitamin C deficiency. Native Americans used the branches to make a steam bath for those suffering from colds, fevers, and for women after childbirth. A poultice made from the wood or leaves was used for rashes, skin irritations, and swellings. Northern white cedar is also prized by wildlife such as white-tailed deer, snowshoe hares, porcupines, and red squirrels, who use it for shelter and browse.

STRIPED MAPLE
Acer pensylvanicum
Maple family (Aceraceae)

Quick ID: Bark green with vertical white stripes; opposite finely double-toothed 5- to 8-inch leaves with 3 shallow lobes, slightly yellowish and hairy beneath; light green flowers in long clusters; winged seeds hanging in long clusters of paired wide-angled samaras (keys)

Height: 10–30 feet

Found in the cool forests of the Northeast, striped maple is a small understory tree named for the distinctive vertical white stripes on the green bark of young trees. Older trees have reddish-brown bark. The green and white stripes allow the tree to photosynthesize better in shaded conditions. The broad leaves are double-toothed with three lobes and resemble the foot of a goose, leading to the common name of goosefoot maple. The big leaves were sometimes used as toilet paper. In autumn, the showy leaves turn bright yellow, brightening the fall landscape. Striped maple twigs are a favorite of deer and moose as winter browse, leading to the common name moosewood. The similar mountain maple (*A. spicatum*) has smaller leaves with coarser teeth on the edges and lacks the white stripes on the bark of striped maple.

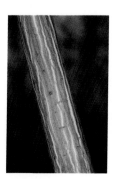

Bark of striped maple   *Mountain maple*   *Fall leaves of mountain maple*

RED MAPLE
Acer rubrum
Maple family (Aceraceae)
Quick ID: Opposite leaves with saw-toothed edges, 3 to 5 lobes and relatively shallow notches between lobes, whitish below; stems and twigs reddish; bark of older trees dark with thin flaky ridges; red clustered flowers; reddish paired forked keys (samaras)

Height: 60–90 feet

Red maple is the most common species of maple in Acadia. This tree is especially appreciated in mid- to late October, when the scarlet red leaves explode with color against the yellows and browns of other autumn leaves. Red maple is able to survive in a wide range of soil and habitat types, but it thrives in wet soil and is often found along the edges of swamps and other wetlands. Widely known in New England as the source of its famous maple syrup, the sugar maple (*A. saccharum*) is also found here, but is not as common as the red maple. Although it does not produce as much as the sugar maple, the sap of red maple was also used to make maple syrup. The boiled inner bark was also used to make blue, purple, and black dyes for fabrics. Ink was made from an infusion of iron sulphate to the tannin from the bark.

Fruits of red maple

Sugar maple

155

AMERICAN MOUNTAIN ASH
Sorbus americana
Rose family (Rosaceae)
Quick ID: Alternate compound leaves with 11 to 17 pointed, toothed leaflets; flat white flower clusters; bright red berries

Height: 15–30 feet

American mountain ash is a small tree that is best recognized in the fall, when the clusters of fire engine red berries command attention. Many birds such as American robins, cedar waxwings, and juncos gorge themselves on the ripe berries in fall. White-tailed deer browse on the leaves and twigs. Although the berries are very tart, they sweeten after a frost and were used to make jellies and wines and were cooked with meat. Even though "ash" is in the common name and the leaves do resemble the shape of ash leaves, it is not related. The leaves of ash trees such as white ash (*Fraxinus americana*) and black ash (*F. nigra*) are opposite rather than alternate. Accidentally introduced in the 1990s, the emerald ash borer (*Agrilus planipennis*), an invasive wood-boring beetle, is destroying ash trees throughout the United States and Canada, where efforts are underway in an attempt to halt its

spread. This destructive insect introduced from Asia may also affect the cultural traditions of the Wabanaki people, who use the wood of the black ash tree to weave beautiful baskets and create other artwork.

Chokecherry

Leaves of chokecherry

PIN CHERRY
Prunus pensylvanica
Rose family (Rosaceae)

Quick ID: Thin leaves, 1.5–4.25 inches; flat-topped clusters of white flowers; dark red 0.25-inch fruit; shiny reddish bark

Height: 16–49 feet

Pin cherry trees are native to most of the eastern states and north into Canada. It is known by many common names, including fire cherry, bird cherry, pigeon cherry, and wild red cherry. The fruits are enjoyed by birds and small mammals, which spread the seeds in their droppings. The even smaller chokecherry (*P. virginiana*) has flowers and fruits in long clusters. The inner seed of the astringent fruit of chokecherry is poisonous, as are the leaves.

QUAKING ASPEN
Populus tremuloides
Willow family (Salicaceae)
Quick ID: Deciduous; broad, heart-shaped to round 1- to 3-inch leaves with finely toothed margins; leaf stems 1.5–3 inches; flowers in 1- to 3-inch drooping spikes called catkins; smooth, whitish-gray bark, often with dark scars

Height: 40–75 feet

The most animated tree in Acadia, the leaves of quaking aspen respond to the slightest breeze by fluttering like green butterfly wings on the branch. Sometimes called trembling aspen, the leaves are attached with flexible flat stems that are attached at right angles to the leaf blade. Aspen roots spread laterally underground, producing vertical shoots called suckers. Genetically identical to the parent tree, the young shoots grow into clones, with many members sharing the same root system. Since quaking aspens are all one organism, the leaves turn color in fall at one time, creating patches of brilliant yellows and oranges. Also found in the park, bigtooth aspen (*P. grandidentata*) has coarser teeth on the leaves.

Seeds

Acorns of northern red oak

NORTHERN RED OAK
Quercus rubra
Beech family (Fagaceae)
Quick ID: Leaves dull green, hairless, 7–9 lobes
with bristlelike tips; dark bark furrowed with shiny
stripes

Height: 70–80 feet

Only two species of oak are found in Acadia, the
northern red oak and the smaller scrub or bear oak
(Q. ilicifolia). Northern red oak is one of the most
common forest trees in New England and is valued
for its pleasing reddish-white wood that is used to
make furniture, flooring, and for other purposes.

Bear oak

The acorns are eaten by a wide variety of animals, including black bears, white-tailed deer, and squirrels.
The genus name for all oaks is *Quercus*. The species name, *rubra*, means "red." The leaves turn brick-red
in fall before dropping to the forest floor for the winter. Scrub or bear oak is an uncommon small shrubby
oak whose range extends in the East from North Carolina into Maine, with a few locations in Canada. The
egg-shaped acorns of scrub oak are short with a saucer-shaped cap and are very bitter, but bears, deer, and
squirrels will eat them. The acorns are a favorite food of wild turkeys.

Trunks of paper birch

PAPER BIRCH
Betula papyrifera
Birch family (Betulaceae)
Quick ID: Chalky white bark with horizontal lines; 2- to 4-inch doubly toothed triangular leaves with 5–9 veins on each side; flowers in separate male and female catkins

Height: 50–75 feet

Easily recognizable, paper birch gets its name from the white papery bark that peels away from the truck in thin sheets that are pinkish inside. This medium sized tree is also known as white birch or canoe birch. The peeled bark has a high oil content, making it waterproof, and it was used to build famed birchbark canoes and for other building purposes. Strips of bark were also used like paper to write on and to bind a broken bone. Young saplings are flexible and capable of bending under the weight of snow and ice. Wildlife including white-tailed deer, snowshoe hares, and moose browse on the twigs. Birds such as redpolls and small mammals eat the catkins. Leaves turn golden yellow in fall. Paper birch is the state tree of nearby New Hampshire. Until recently, the very similar mountain paper birch (*B. cordifolia*) was considered to be a variety of paper

Bark of paper birch

birch. This species is also known as heartleaf birch, which refers to the heart shape at the base of the leaf.

Mountain paper birch

Bark of mountain paper birch

Bark of gray birch

GRAY BIRCH
Betula populifolia
Birch family (Betulaceae)
Quick ID: Grayish-white chalky bark; multiple trunks; doubly toothed triangular leaves with long pointed tip; 2- to 3.5-inch male flowers hang down in catkins; 0.5-inch female flowers are erect

Height: 20–40 feet

Gray birch is a common tree in the northern United States and Canada. It is a relatively small, bushy tree, typically up to 30 feet tall. The leaves are triangular, double-toothed, and taper to a point. The leaves turn soft, pale yellow in fall, dancing in the cooling breeze on thin stalks. The flexible branches bend to the ground when weighed down with heavy snow. Yellow birch (*B. alleghaniensis*) is much taller, reaching up to 100 feet tall. Also known as silver birch, the bark is shiny yellow or silvery gray. The bark separates into papery, curly strips that turn reddish brown.

Yellow birch

Bark of yellow birch

AMERICAN BEECH
Fagus grandifolia
Beech family (Fagaceae)
Quick ID: Smooth light gray bark; dark green, glossy, toothed, egg-shaped 1- to 5-inch leaves; triangular nuts in prickly burs; long, thin cigar-shaped buds

Height: 60–98 feet

Beeches are tall, beautiful shade trees with a rounded crown and spreading horizontal branches. Held in prickly burs, the edible beechnuts were stored for use during the long winter months. The nuts are eaten by many species of wildlife, including wild turkeys, foxes, raccoons, squirrels, and white-tailed deer. The wood is used for tool handles and furniture. The leaves turn yellowish orange in autumn, adding to the stunning palette of the Maine woods in fall. Unfortunately, beech trees are under siege by several diseases and pests. Beech bark disease occurs when the European beech scale insect (*Cryptococcus fagisuga*) damages the bark, which is in turn infected by two species of fungi. The leaves are being attacked by a nematode and a weevil.

Beech leaf disease

WESTERN POISON IVY
Toxicodendron rydbergii
Sumac family (Anacardiaceae)
Quick ID: Shrub; 3 leaflets with pointed tips, each 2- to 4.5-inches long
Length: 1–4 feet

Although poison ivy is not common in Acadia, visitors to the park should be aware that it is found here, especially in rocky places, shrubby areas, and along fence lines. Fortunately, with its characteristic leaves of three, this plant is easy to identify. Poison ivy contains urushiol, an oil that causes an itchy, blistering skin rash in 80 percent of people. If you do happen to come in contact with poison ivy, gently wash the area with soap and water as soon as possible. Another even less common species, eastern poison ivy (*T. radicans*) is also found in the park, typically as a creeping vine. The genus name, *Toxicodendron*, comes from the Greek words *toxico* and *dendron*, for "poisonous tree."

Close-up of speckled
alder leaf

SPECKLED ALDER
Alnus incana
Birch family (Betulaceae)

Quick ID: Bark speckled with horizontal white warty bumps (lenticels); leaves egg-shaped, pointed at the tip and rounded at the base with edges double-toothed, underside dull green with conspicuous crossveins extending between secondary veins; flowers in catkins

Height: 6–12 feet   Bloom season: April–May

Speckled alder is a medium-sized shrub with multiple stems. Growing in wet areas, the shrub provides cover for wildlife and is browsed by white-tailed deer and moose. Sometimes called green alder, the leaves of mountain alder (*A. viridis*) have leaves with finely toothed edges rather than the coarsely toothed edges of speckled alder. Also, the underside of the leaves of mountain alder has crossveins that are not continuous between the parallel secondary veins.

Close-up of mountain alder leaf

Mountain alder

BAR HARBOR JUNIPER
Juniperus horizontalis
Cypress family (Cupressaceae)
Quick ID: Evergreen; blue-green scalelike leaves when mature, prickly and awl-like when young; blue seed cones

Height: 0.8–12 inches   Bloom season: March–April

Also called creeping juniper, Bar Harbor juniper is native to northern New England. A cultivar of creeping juniper, the Bar Harbor juniper was found at Mount Desert on the rocky coast in open dry areas. The similar ground juniper (*J. communis*) is variable in form, either prostrate or tall shrublike. The fruit are berrylike cones called juniper berries. After eating the berries, birds distribute the seeds to other areas. The astringent juniper berries are used to flavor meats and sauces and are used for the characteristic flavor of gin. Juniper berries are also used to treat fungal infections.

Ground juniper

NORTHERN BUSH HONEYSUCKLE
Diervilla lonicera
Bush Honeysuckle family (Diervillaceae)
Quick ID: Yellow funnel-shaped flowers in 3s; opposite green oval leaves

Height: 1–4 feet   Bloom season: May–August

The funnel-shaped yellow flowers of northern bush honeysuckle are very similar to the flowers of true honeysuckles. Bumblebees, hummingbirds, and butterflies love the sweet nectar the flowers provide. The dark green leaves turn yellow to orange then reddish to purple in the fall. Native Americans used the leaves medicinally as a diuretic.

BEARBERRY
Arctostaphylos uva-ursi
Heath family (Ericaceae)

Quick ID: Spreading undercover shrub; alternate, spoon-shaped leaves; pink bell-shaped flowers; bright red fruit

Height: 6–12 inches   Bloom season: May–July

Bearberry is a short spreading shrub found in dry rocky places and on mountaintops. Bearberry is also known by the common name kinnikinnic, which comes from an Algonquin word meaning "that which is mixed." The leaves were dried and mixed with the leaves of other plants to be used as a tobacco substitute. Leaves were also used medicinally to treat urinary disorders and hemorrhoids. The bright red berries (drupes) are mealy but were often dried and used in food mixtures. The fruits spoil slowly and often remain on the branches into spring, when they are eaten by birds and bears and other mammals. The leaves are the larval food plant for the hoary elfin butterfly (*Callophrys polios*).

SHEEP LAUREL
Kalmia angustifolia
Heath family (Ericaceae)

Quick ID: Evergreen narrow, leathery, oblong, 1.5- to 2-inch leaves dark green above, pale underneath; bowl-shaped deep pink flowers growing along the stem in clusters

Height: 1–3 feet   Bloom season: June–August

Sheep laurel is a common shrub in both open forest edges and wetlands. The spectacular crimson-pink blossoms of sheep laurel are composed of five petals fused together into a shallow bowl. The long anthers are lodged within the petals until a bee or other insect brushes against them, causing them to spring outward and fling pollen onto the bee. All parts of sheep laurel are highly toxic and poisonous to mammals. The plant contains a glycoside called andromedotoxin that has led to other common names, including lambkill and sheep kill. Even honey made from the pollen and nectar contains the toxin; it is called "mad honey" and can cause paralysis. The genus, *Kalmia*, is named for Peter Kalm, a Swedish botanist who was a student of Linnaeus. The species name, *angustifolia*, means "narrow leaved." Found only in boggy areas, bog laurel (*K. polifolia*), also known as pale or swamp laurel, has leaves that are white underneath and rolled on the edges.

Bog laurel

BLACK CROWBERRY
Empetrum nigrum
Heath family (Ericaceae)

Quick ID: Evergreen; small pinkish flowers; short needlelike leaves whorled around stem; fruit (drupe) purple, turning black

Height: 4–10 inches   Bloom season: May–June

Black crowberry is named for the small round black fruits called drupes it produces in late summer. Often referred to simply as crowberry, the plant is a low-growing shrub that spreads by creeping, forming large mats. Adapted to harsh climates, crowberry is a plant of the cold northlands and is able to withstand both wind and cold. With circumboreal distribution, it is found in most Northern Hemisphere countries. The acidic fruits are often mixed with more flavorful berries and used to make jelly, pie, juice, and wine. The fruit is also dried and stored to be eaten during the cold winter months. Many animals and birds also enjoy the fruits. A related species, broom crowberry (*Corema conradii*) has flowers and fruits only at the end of the stem; although not common in the park, it can be seen on Ship Harbor Trail.

BLACK HUCKLEBERRY
Gaylussacia baccata
Heath family (Ericaceae)
Quick ID: Pinkish-red urn-shaped clustered flowers; alternate, elliptical 1- to 3-inch leaves covered on both sides with resin dots, underside of leaf yellowish; shiny blue-black fruits (drupes); dark bark, twigs reddish

Height: 1–3 feet   Bloom season: May–June

Black huckleberry is a common shrub in Acadia, often found growing near the shorter lowbush blueberries (*Vaccinium angustifolium*). Dangling in clusters, the urn-shaped flowers hang from branching stems that spread to form dense thickets in sunny areas. The shiny dark bluish-black fruits are sweet edibles, containing small seeds that crackle in your mouth. Hanging upside down, bees and small butterflies nectar at the flowers. Many species of wildlife make use of the shrub, including snowshoe hares, ruffed grouse, wild turkeys, crossbills, and grosbeaks. The leaves turn stunning shades of crimson-orange in the fall. Another shrub with shiny black fruits, black chokeberry (*Aronia melanocarpa*) has five-petaled white flowers with pinkish stamens, but the fruits are very bitter.

Leaf of black huckleberry

Black chokeberry

RHODORA
Rhododendron canadense
Heath family (Ericaceae)
Quick ID: Magenta flowers clustered on stem tip, stamens protruding beyond petals; oval leaves

Height: 1–3 feet   Bloom season: May–June

In Maine, the bright magenta flowers of rhodora bloom before the leaves are fully unfurled. This cheery spring bloomer prefers bogs and poorly drained soils and can be found along wet meadows and fields. Ralph Waldo Emerson sang the praises of this lovely spring shrub in a poem he titled "The Rhodora, on Being Asked, Whence Is the Flower." Rhodora has a very short blooming period, late May into early June, and spring visitors enjoy this lovely flower in bloom. Look for rhodora throughout the park in areas such as Great Meadow, Ship Harbor Trail, and Cadillac Mountain.

LABRADOR TEA
Rhododendron groenlandicum
Heath family (Ericaceae)
Quick ID: Evergreen; white flowers with 5 petals; alternate, oval leathery leaves with rusty woolly hairs underneath, rolled edges; stems with woolly brown hairs

Height: 1–3 feet   Bloom season: May–June

Labrador tea is a shrub of wetlands and bogs in the cool North. The bright white flowers have five petals in clusters. The characteristic leathery leaves curl under along the edges, and if you take a peek underneath you will see the leaf is covered with fuzzy brown hairs. The aromatic leaves were used to make a tea that was used medicinally for colds, stuffy noses, and headaches. In Maine, the bogs in which Labrador tea grows are an important habitat for waterfowl.

LOWBUSH BLUEBERRY
Vaccinium angustifolium
Heath family (Ericaceae)
Quick ID: Pinkish-white bell-shaped flowers; narrow, finely toothed leaves; branched stems in clumps that spread by underground stems; fruit small dark blue berry

Height: 2–24 inches
Bloom season: April–June

Lowbush blueberry, or low sweet blueberry, is a familiar shrub in Acadia and throughout Maine. Full of antioxidants, tiny wild blueberries contain about one-third more anthocyanins than cultivated blueberries. Anthocyanins are responsible for the rich color of the berry and are also high in antioxidants, which help reduce inflammation and have other health benefits. In Maine, fields of blueberries help satisfy the nation's demand for this superfruit; more than 98 percent of the nation's lowbush blueberries are harvested here, and blueberries have become one of the state's important exports. So loved and valued is the wild blueberry, in 1991 it was designated as the official state berry. In 2011 blueberry pie was recognized as the official state dessert. Several other species of blueberry can be found in the park, including highbush blueberry (*V. corymbosum*), which grows up to 6 feet tall in wet areas.

Highbush blueberry

Fruit of mountain cranberry

LARGE CRANBERRY
Vaccinium macrocarpon
Heath family (Ericaceae)
Quick ID: Evergreen; pinkish-white flowers with 5 recurved petals on slender stalks; creeping woody stems; small oblong leathery leaves with blunt tips; fruits red berry

Height: 1–3 feet   Bloom season: June–August

Tiny pinkish-white shooting-star flowers adorn large cranberry shrubs. The flower stamens somewhat resemble the beak of a crane, giving rise to the name cranberry. The tart berries are well known for their use in sauces, jellies, dried fruit, and juice. Small cranberry (*V. oxycoccos*) has smaller leaves and fruits. A low-growing evergreen shrub, mountain cranberry (*V. vitis-idaea*) has tiny pinkish bell-shaped flowers and small rounded evergreen leaves. Known by

Small cranberry

many common names, including lingonberry, the tart bright red berries are cooked and mixed with sugar to make delicious jams, pies, and syrups. Extremely hardy, the berries sweeten if left on the branch through winter.

Mountain cranberry

Fruit of large cranberry

SWEETFERN
Comptonia peregrina
Bayberry family (Myricaceae)
Quick ID: Fernlike foliage with flattened, deeply notched 3- to 6-inch leaves; woody stem and branches; male flowers in catkins, female flowers reddish becoming yellow-green burrs that resemble galls

Height: 2–4 feet   Bloom season: April–June

Interspersed between the lush world of ferns is a shrub that that so resembles a fern that most hikers assume it *is* a fern. Even though this mysterious plant resembles a fern, is it actually a shrub with sweet smelling foliage that has earned it the name "sweetfern." A native shrub of eastern North America, it grows widely in disturbed sunny areas. The species name, *peregrina*, means a "traveler" or "wanderer." The genus, *Comptonia*, honors Henry Compton (1632–1713) a bishop in London, England, who was also a botanist. A part of Compton's job was to select ministers to travel overseas to attend to the spiritual welfare of British overseas territories. He skillfully selected ministers with a knowledge of botany, who sent him around a thousand specimens and seeds from the New World, the Caribbean, Africa, and India, many of which he was able to grow in his garden. Famous early botanist John Banister was one of these overseas ministers who added much knowledge of the plant world.

NORTHERN BAYBERRY

Morella pensylvanica
Bayberry family (Myricaceae)
Quick ID: Rounded shrub; glossy, gray-green
egg-shaped leaves; small flowers in 0.5-inch
catkins appearing before leaves; fruits round, hard,
bluish-white berries

Flowers of northern bayberry

Height: 3–12 feet   Bloom season: April–May

When crushed, the fragrant leaves of northern
bayberry release the pleasantly familiar scent of
bayberry candles. The small clusters of hard, round
bluish-white berries remain on the stem into winter
and are eaten by birds such as ruffed grouse.
To make candles, the hard waxy berries were
gathered, boiled, and then allowed to cool. After
the wax solidified, it was removed to make fragrant
bayberry candles. A similar shrub in the Bayberry
family, sweet gale (*Myrica gale*) has fruits that are
brownish-red achenes. A boreal plant, mountain

Sweet gale

holly (*Ilex mucronata*) has a similar leaf shape to both of these shrubs. The inconspicuous white flowers
give rise to bright, eye-catching red berrylike drupes in the fall. Winterberry holly (*I. verticillata*) is widely
planted for its attractive bright red fruits, which birds eat but are poisonous to humans.

Mountain holly

Winterberry

BEACH ROSE
Rosa rugosa
Rose family (Rosaceae)

Quick ID: Large showy rosy pink or white petals with yellow center; leathery deeply veined leaves toothed and wrinkled; stems with dense, straight prickles; 1-inch fruits round, red rose "hips"

Height: 3–5 feet   Bloom season: June–July

Acadia's dramatic shorelines are decorated with the heady, fragrant blooms of beach roses, which grow as spreading shrubs on the rocky coast. It may be hard to believe that something so beautiful, so fragrant, so abundant could be an unwanted plant in Maine, but beach rose is considered a non-native invasive plant. Introduced into North America in the 1770s from Asia, it is now a common feature along the shores of New England. The leathery leaves of this rose are coarsely toothed and appear wrinkled, leading to the species name, *rugosa*, which is Latin for "wrinkled." You can see this rose near Seawall Picnic Area, along Ocean Path, and Blueberry Hill on the Schoodic Loop Road. Other common names include rugosa rose and salt spray rose. Several other species of roses can be found in the park, including bristly rose (*R. nitida*) and Virginia rose (*R. virginiana*).

Close-up of beach rose

Virginia rose

Steeplebush

MEADOWSWEET
Spiraea alba
Rose family (Rosaceae)
Quick ID: Tiny white flowers in cone shape at the end of branches; glossy, narrow leaves sharply toothed, hairless; small brown, dry fruit

Height: 3–4 feet   Bloom season: June–August

Sometimes called narrowleaf meadowsweet, this shrub is found in boggy areas. The white flowers form cone-like spires at the end of the stem. Steeplebush (*S. tomentosa*) has deep pink flowers in spire-like clusters at the top of the stem. Sometimes called rosy meadowsweet, this tall shrub is common in boggy wetlands. The leaves have brownish hairs on the underside. Both plants were used as a healing drink. An infusion of leaves and stems was used as a medicinal tea.

NORTHERN WILD RAISIN
Viburnum cassinoides
Viburnum family (Viburnaceae)

Quick ID: White flowers in flat-topped clusters on stalks; opposite, leathery 4- to 8-inch-long heart-shaped finely toothed leaves; dark purple fruits

Height: 6–10 feet   Bloom season: June–August

Northern wild raisin is a medium-sized shrub with flat clusters of white starry flowers. In fall the red berrylike drupes turn blue-black and wrinkled and look somewhat like raisins. The fruits have a large seed inside but have been used for food. Witherod is another common name for this shrub, in reference to the word "wei" or "withe," which refers to a slender, flexible stem. The berrylike drupes are not a favorite of wildlife, but birds such as rose-breasted grosbeaks will eat them in winter. Hobblebush (*V. lantanoides*) is a similar shrub with flat white flowers and red berries that turn blue. The branches of hobblebush, or witch hobble as it is sometimes called, bend and take root along the ground, forming loops that may trip, or "hobble," unwary hikers.

Fruits of northern wild raisin

Hobblebush

FRAGRANT WATER LILY
Nymphaea odorata
Water Lily family (Nymphaeaceae)
Quick ID: Aquatic; fragrant white flowers with spiral petals and yellow stamens; flat green 4- to 12-inch leaves, notched and split to the stem, purple underneath; long underwater stems to 5 or 6 feet long

Height: 3–5 inches   Bloom season: June–September

Floating leaves of fragrant water lily float in quiet ponds in the park. Native to eastern North America, the showy fragrant white flowers attract bees, beetles, and flies. The roots were used as a poultice for wounds and swellings. Beavers, muskrats, and turtles eat the plants. Yellow pond lily (*Nuphar variegata*) has cup-shaped yellow flowers.

Leaves of fragrant water lily

Yellow pond lily

SKUNK CABBAGE
Symplocarpus foetidus
Arum family (Araceae)

Quick ID: Tiny yellow flowers on rounded spike (spadix); mottled green to purple shell-like 3- to 6-inch sheath (spathe); large, broad, veined dark green leaves to 1 foot wide and up to 2 feet long on stalk rising from ground

Height: 1–3 feet   Bloom season: February–April

Wafting through the sharp winter air, the fetid, rotting-meat aroma of blooming skunk cabbage is irresistible to carrion flies and other insects that may be active in late winter. Unique in the flower world, skunk cabbage can generate heat up to 68 toasty degrees, even when the ambient temperature falls below zero. This process, called thermogenesis, can melt snow around the plant and allows the flower to bloom in cold weather. Snails and beetles are also attracted to the plant's warmth, seeking refuge within its protective sheath. Skunk cabbage contains the chemical calcium oxalate, which burns if eaten, causing swelling of the throat and mouth. Even so, after having been cooked in several water baths, the leaves have been historically used for food. During the mid-1800s it was utilized as a medicine called dracontium, which was prescribed for respiratory and nervous conditions. The dried leaves were also used for swellings and headaches. Found in boggy wet areas, you can see the large leaves of skunk cabbage along Wonderland Trail.

BLUEBEAD LILY
Clintonia borealis
Lily family (Liliaceae)

Quick ID: Clusters of 3–8 nodding yellow flowers with 6 reflexed petals and protruding stamens; 4- to 16-inch-long stalks; 2–4 shiny, oval, slender leaves, 5–12 inches long; fruits dark blue berries

Height: 6–16 inches   Bloom season: May–July

Bluebead lily is named for the bright blue berries that adorn the plant in fall. This member of the lily family is also called yellow clintonia, honoring not only the yellow flowers but also DeWitt Clinton, the botany-loving governor of New York from 1769 to 1828. Spreading by underground rhizomes, colonies of these stunning beauties are pollinated by bees, bumblebees, and butterflies. Native Americans used the leaves to make a poultice that was applied to wounds and infections. Even though the blue berries look enticing, they are somewhat toxic and can cause mild gastric upset if ingested. Very slow growing, it may take ten to twelve years for this plant to flower. Please do not pick these or any other flowers in the park.

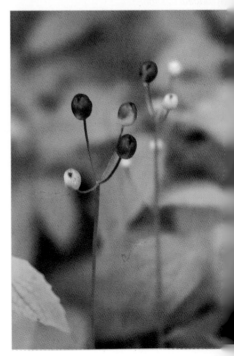

PINK LADY'S SLIPPER
Cypripedium acaule
Orchid family (Orchidaceae)
Quick ID: Single pink pouch-shaped flower with slit in front; leafless stalk; 2 basal leaves, opposite, oval with grooves

Height: 6–15 inches   Bloom season: May–June

What a lovely sight it is in May to see pink lady's slippers gracing the trails and partially shaded banks in moist forests in the park. The plant thrives in dry acidic soils, especially in coniferous habitats. The unusual pouch shape of the blossoms reminds you a bit of moccasins, giving rise to another common name, moccasin flower. Pink lady's slippers are in the orchid family along with their rare cousin, the showy or queen's lady's slipper (*C. reginae*), which grows in seepage swamps and wet forests. These orchids are dependent on particular fungi in the soil for survival. This mutualistic association is called a mycorrhizal relationship. If the flower is not allowed to complete its life cycle,

White morph

t will not regenerate. It is against park rules to pick flowers in the national park, especially wildflowers as special as lady's slippers. In some areas in Maine, such as Baxter State Park, the dominant color of pink lady's slippers is the nearly white form.

BLUE FLAG
Iris versicolor
Iris family (Iridaceae)

Quick ID: Violet-blue 2.5- to 4-inch flowers with 3 petals and 3 petallike downcurved sepals that have yellow veins; arching swordlike leaves in bunch from underground rhizome; 2- to 3-foot-tall stalk

Height: 2–3 feet   Bloom season: June–August

Growing in wet meadows, the showy violet-blue iris-like flowers of blue flag, or harlequin blueflag, are distinctly marked with yellow stripes on the sepals. These colorful stripes serve as nectar guides to channel pollinators into the nectar. The Old English word for rush or reed is "flagge," leading to the common name blue flag, as is shares the same wetland habitat. Even though the rhizome is poisonous, it has been used to treat wounds, sores, and burns. In Greek mythology, Iris was the goddess of the rainbow. Whenever a rainbow appeared, Iris was bringing a message from Olympus to someone on Earth. Another large purple flower that grows in wetlands, pickerelweed (*Pontederia cordata*) has a spike of flowers and large heart-shaped leaves.

Pickerelweed

Close-up of pickerelweed flower

BEACH PEA
Lathyrus japonicus var. maritimus
Legume family (Fabaceae)

Quick ID: Creeping vine; pinkish to violet flowers in stalked clusters; waxy oval leaflets along the stem with twining tendrils at the tip; fruit encased in a 2-inch pealike pod

Length: 4–5 feet   Bloom season: June–August

Remarkably adapted to harsh conditions along the ocean's edge, beach pea has waxy leaves that help it survive the hot temperatures without drying out. This low, sprawling vine occurs in rocky and gravelly coastal areas and salt marshes in the park, such as those found at Seawall Picnic Area. With a hard coating, the seeds of beach pea, or sea vetchling, can stay viable in water for up to five years, giving the plant an optimum opportunity to spread to coastlines throughout much of the world. The seeds and leaves are known to be edible. However, the seeds contain a toxic protein, which if eaten in large quantities can cause a nervous system disease called lathyrism. Bees pollinate the flowers. The original genus name, *Lathyros*, comes from a word meaning "passionate," as the plant was thought to be an aphrodisiac.

BIGLEAF LUPINE
Lupinus polyphyllus
Legume family (Fabaceae)
Quick ID: Purple, blue, or pinkish spikes of pealike flowers; 9–17 leaflets on fan-shaped leaf; 1- to 2-inch brown, woolly fruit pod

Height: 3–5 feet   Bloom season: May–July

Showstopping candy-stick pillars of pastel flowers line roadways and open areas in Maine. Commonly known as blue-pod or garden lupine, this lovely flower is native to the

Pacific Northwest. It was introduced into Maine as a landscape plant but quickly spread outside the garden boundaries. Unfortunately, this non-native beauty crowds out native plants that typically inhabit the forest edges and roadsides. Even though this newcomer to the area may be taking over delicate native habitat, the showy flowers add dramatic beauty to the landscape. The nectar-rich flowers attract native bees, bumblebees, other insects, and ruby-throated hummingbirds.

THREE-TOOTHED CINQUEFOIL
Sibbaldiopsis tridentata
Rose family (Rosaceae)

Quick ID: Low-growing evergreen with slightly woody stem; white flowers with 5 rounded petals, 13 or more projecting stamens; leaves with 3 leaflets, each with 3 rounded teeth at tip

Height: 1–10 inches   Bloom season: June–August

The five white petals of three-toothed cinquefoil surround a starry center, and the tips of the evergreen leaves are serrated with three tips leading to the common name. Three-toothed cinquefoil is one of the plants being used to restore the subalpine vegetation on damaged areas on Cadillac Mountain. The plant is able to withstand the extreme climate conditions on the summit of this mountain that stands 1,500 feet above Frenchman Bay. About 16 percent of the areas that once supported unique plants have been eroded to bare rock. This massive park effort has been supported by Friends of Acadia, Native Plant Trust, and Schoodic Institute. You can do your part to save these unique sites by watching where you place your feet and staying on existing trails to avoid trampling small plants and lichens.

ROUND-LEAVED SUNDEW
Drosera rotundifolia
Sundew family (Droseraceae)

Quick ID: Flower with 5 white petals on one side of stalk; leaf blades broader than long on a long stalk, each leaf covered with reddish, sticky glandular hairs

Height: 4–9 inches   Bloom season: July–August

Hikers on Acadia trails enjoy the stunning scenery and beautiful mountain views but may not be aware of the carnivorous plants growing along the trail close to their hiking boots. Growing in boggy areas, round-leaved sundews quietly wait for an unsuspecting insect to jump onto their leaves covered with tiny, sticky hairs. Once the insect lands on a leaf, the leaf curls around it, trapping the insect in those sticky hairs. Living in a nitrogen-deficient boggy environment, the sundew secretes enzymes to digest the insect, which provides the plant with needed minerals and nitrogen. Spatulate leaved sundew (*D. intermedia*) has leaf blades that are longer than they are broad. Look for sundews along the Jordan Pond Path.

Spatulate leaved sundew

Flower of spatulate leaved sundew

Spatulate leaved sundew

BUNCHBERRY
Chamaepericlymenum canadense
Dogwood family (Cornaceae)

Quick ID: Opposite, veined, egg-shaped leaves in whorl of 4–6; 4 white bracts that resemble petals; cluster of red berrylike drupes

Height: 4–8 inches   Bloom season: May–June

Forming thick carpets of flowers under trees in moist, acidic soils, bunchberry, or dwarf dogwood, is the smallest members of the dogwood family. Four white petallike bracts surround the tiny yellowish-green true flowers in the center. The white bracts help attract pollinators to the insignificant flowers. On average, more than twenty tiny flowers in the center are pollinated by bees, flies, and other insects. These minute flowers have an amazing pollination technique. When an insect brushes against the tiny petal, it releases the pollen-tipped anther on the end of a springy stem called a filament. This flings the pollen upward at a rate of up to 24,000 meters per second. In late summer and fall, bunchberry presents a bunch of red berries, hence the common name. The bland berries can be eaten raw, but normally are cooked and used in a sauce. The leaves turn reddish purple in fall.

STARFLOWER
Trientalis borealis
Primrose family (Primulaceae)

Quick ID: 1–4 white star-shaped flowers with 5–9 petals on threadlike stalks, yellow tipped anthers; lance-shaped, pointed leaves in a whorl

Height: 3.9–7.8 inches   Bloom season: May–June

In the warming temperatures of early spring, starflowers grace the understory of Acadia's awakening forests. The brilliant white petals glow brightly like tiny stars against the dark green whorled leaves. Another early bloomer, Canada mayflower (*Maianthemum canadense*) is a widespread low-growing plant that often forms colonies in the understory. Canada mayflower is sometimes called false lily of the valley, as it somewhat resembles a small American lily of the valley (*Convallaria pseudomajalis*), which is endemic to the Southern Appalachians. An upright zigzag stem holds two glossy green leaves topped with a cluster of tiny white starlike flowers. The fruits that stay on the stems into spring provide food for birds such as grouse, which help spread the seeds away from the parent plant.

Canada mayflower

NORTHERN PITCHER PLANT
Sarracenia purpurea
Pitcher Plant family (Sarraceniaceae)
Quick ID: Deep maroon nodding flat disk flowers on long, smooth stem; funnel-shaped leaves with downward-pointing hairs

Height: 8–24 inches   Bloom season: May–August

Growing only in sphagnum bogs and marshes, northern pitcher plant is a carnivorous plant that traps and digests flying and crawling insects. The stiff, downward-pointing hairs help prevent insects from escaping. The upright pitcher-shaped leaves collect rainwater and dew. The plant is pollinated by the pitcher plant fly (*Fletcherimyia fletcheri*). The larvae live in the water and dine on some of the trapped insects. Northern pitcher plants were used medicinally by Native Americans to treat smallpox. It has since been shown that the plant contains antiviral properties that inhibit the replication of the virus that causes smallpox.

WINTERGREEN
Gaultheria procumbens
Heath family (Ericaceae)

Quick ID: Evergreen, shiny, thick, oval 1- to 2-inch leaves; creeping stem; white, nodding, bell-shaped flowers; red berries

Height: 2–6 inches   Bloom season: July–August

The thick oval leaves of this small evergreen plant lie low against the forest floor throughout the park. Blooming in summer, the small white bell-shaped flowers hang beneath the leaves and are often overlooked by hikers. Sometimes described as "sealing-wax red," the dry berries that replace the flowers are often more noticeable, especially as they often last into the winter. Often called eastern teaberry, the leaves were used to make a pleasant wintergreen-flavored tea. Early colonists used the tea medicinally to treat the aches and pains of arthritis. Chipmunks and squirrels enjoy the tasty berries in winter, and deer browse on the leaves. In 1999 wintergreen was designated the official state herb of Maine. Another low-creeping wildflower, trailing arbutus (*Epigaea repens*) has clusters of five-petaled pink to white flowers that bloom in early spring.

GHOST PIPE
Monotropa uniflora
Heath family (Ericaceae)

Quick ID: Translucent waxy white flower and stem; nodding urn-shaped flowers blacken with age

Height: 2–10 inches   Bloom season: June–September

Catching the eye of hikers through rich woods in the park, the waxy white flowers of ghost pipe rise mysteriously through the leaf litter. A strange looking but amazing little flower, ghost pipe, or ghost plant, has found a way to survive even though it lacks the ability to perform photosynthesis. Without the ability to produce its own food, ghost pipe leaches sugars from a fungus in the soil. The fungus, either a *Russula* or a *Lactarius*, forms a mutually beneficial relationship with tree roots, which supply the fungus with sugars; in return, the fungus helps the tree absorb water and minerals. This complex triangled relationship enables the ghost pipe to survive in the dense understory of rich woods, where little sunlight reaches the forest floor. The plant turns black with age and dissolves into gelatinous goo.

ORANGE HAWKWEED
Pilosella aurantiaca
Aster family (Asteraceae)
Quick ID: Bright orange dandelion-like 1-inch flowers with toothed square tips, flowers in clusters of 2–25; leafless stem with hairs; hairy leaves in a rosette at the base of the plant; seeds with fuzzy white tuft in ball

Height: 6–24 inches   Bloom season: May–September

Native to the alpine regions of Europe, the bright orange flowers of orange hawkweed line roadsides and disturbed areas. It spreads easily by underground rhizomes or by windblown seeds. In some states it is listed as a noxious weed. Hawkweeds get their name from the legend that hawks get their keen sight by eating the sap of the plant. The related mouse-ear hawkweed (*P. officinarum*) produces similar flowers, but they are lemon yellow.

Mouse-ear hawkweed

NEW YORK ASTER
Symphyotrichum novi-belgii
Aster family (Asteraceae)

Quick ID: Purple to lavender 1- to 3-inch flowers with yellow center; alternate, narrow leaves clasping stem; reddish stem with fine hairs

Height: 3–5 feet   Bloom season: July–October

At least twelve species of asters can be found in Acadia, sporting purple to white flowers in late summer and fall. The word "aster" comes from the Greek word for star. The lavender petals are not actually petals but florets that surround central disk flowers. Butterflies and other insects fill up with nectar from the central disk flowers. Several species of asters, including New York aster, are the host plant for the caterpillar of the pearl crescent butterfly. Northern flat-topped aster (*Doellingeria umbellata*), another common aster in Acadia, has a large cluster of flowers with white rays.

Northern flat-topped aster

Flower of northern flat-topped aster

TALL GOLDENROD
Solidago altissima
Aster family (Asteraceae)

Quick ID: Plumelike clusters of flowers with 9–15 yellow rays; stem downy; narrow, some toothed leaves with downy underneath

Height: 1–5 feet   Bloom season: August–October

Wildflower meadows spring to life in late summer with tall waving goldenrods painting the meadow bright yellow with their blossoms. Some goldenrods are plumelike like tall goldenrod; others are wand-like, such as Rand's goldenrod (*S. randii*) or downy goldenrod (*S. puberula*). Grass-leaved goldenrod (*Euthamia graminifolia*) is a flat-topped species. The pollen grains are large and heavy, and since they are not carried by the wind, the plants rely on bees, butterflies, and other insects for pollination. Goldenrod has been blamed for the allergies of fall, but the itchy eyes and runny noses are from the pollen of common ragweed (*Ambrosia artemisiifolia*), which blooms at the same time.

Rand's goldenrod

Downy goldenrod

Grass-leaved goldenrod

WILD SARSAPARILLA
Aralia nudicaulis
Ginseng family (Araliaceae)

Quick ID: Round clusters of 1- to 2-inch greenish-white flowers on leafless stalk, flowers under leaves; whorl of 3 leaves in groups of 5 finely serrated leaflets 3–5 inches long and 2 inches wide; leaves on separate stem from flowers; blue-black berries

Height: 8–20 inches   Bloom season: May–July

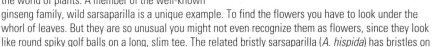

Unexpected characteristics add rich diversity to the world of plants. A member of the well-known ginseng family, wild sarsaparilla is a unique example. To find the flowers you have to look under the whorl of leaves. But they are so unusual you might not even recognize them as flowers, since they look like round spiky golf balls on a long, slim tee. The related bristly sarsaparilla (*A. hispida*) has bristles on the stem and the golf ball–like flowers are above the leaves. In late summer, the flowers of both species are replaced by dark blue berries that are very astringent but have been used to make jelly and wine. Native Americans used an infusion of the roots as a tonic to strengthen the blood and for childhood pneumonia and teething. The root was also used to decrease pain and swelling of sores and burns.

Leaves of bristly sarsaparilla

Fruit of bristly sarsaparilla

SWEETGRASS
Hierochloe odorata
Grass family (Poaceae)
Quick ID: Flat bright green leaves with reddish color at the base; spreads by creeping, underground stems called rhizomes

Height: 6–35 inches

A lovely name for a simple plant, sweetgrass is a fragrant grass with hints of vanilla-scented leaves. Many Indigenous people in New England and Canada traditionally use sweetgrass as a material for basketweaving. Playing an important role in Wabanaki culture, it was gathered growing along the edges of wetlands then dried in the sun. After drying, it was soaked to make it pliable, then often braided into thick threads to be used in weaving mats, containers, and baskets. Known as the "hair of Mother Earth," this grass was an important part of cultural and economic survival for the Wabanaki people. In the mid- to late 1800s and the turn of the twentieth century, these talented artisans made beautiful baskets with black ash and sweetgrass to sell to tourists who summered in Maine. You can see examples of these handicrafts at the Abbe Museum in Bar Harbor.

Quick ID for Grasses, Sedges, and Rushes

	Family	Stem
Grasses	Poaceae	Jointed, usually round
Sedges	Cyperaceae	Lacking joints, usually triangular
Rushes	Juncaceae	Lacking joints, rounded and solid

SALTMEADOW CORDGRASS
Spartina patens
Grass family (Poaceae)
Quick ID: 0.5- to 1-inch droopy, wiry leaves; upper side shiny dark green, lower surface rough; inflorescence with 2–10 2-inch-long spikelets

Height: 1–4 feet

From Newfoundland to Florida on the east coast of North America, large colonies of saltmeadow cordgrass form in sandy areas and tidal marshes. Cordgrass grows from rhizomes, which are underground horizontal stems with roots growing from them. Grasses are flowering plants and with more than 10,000 species, the grass family (Poaceae) is the fifth-largest family of plants. Grasses have jointed stems, while the stems of sedges and rushes lack joints. The stems of sedges have edges; those of rushes are round.

SCIRPUS BULRUSH
Scirpus sp.
Sedge family (Cyperaceae)
Quick ID: 3-angled stems; flat grasslike leaves; greenish or brownish flowers in clusters of small spikelets

Height: 8–47+ inches

Scirpus is a genus of sedges with many common names, including bulrush and wood club-rush. These sedges are common in wetlands and have a variety of flowering head shapes, from ball-like to graceful nodding tops. About six *Scirpus* species can be found in Acadia.

TUSSOCK COTTONSEDGE
Eriophorum vaginatum
Sedge family (Cyperaceae)
Quick ID: Triangular stem; tufts of narrow hairlike leaves with single leaf sheath; inflorescence dense, tufted, solitary spike

Height: 12–23.6 inches

Although the name cottongrass is wonderfully descriptive, the plant is neither cotton nor grass. If you look carefully at the stem of cottongrasses, you will notice they have a triangular stem, characteristic of sedges. The cottony tops are featherlike and attached to the seed, which assists with wind dispersal. About twenty species of cottongrass can be found in northern and boreal areas worldwide, with about five of these species in Acadia. One of these species, tussock cottonsedge, is also called hare's tail cottongrass, as from a distance it looks like fields of hares hopping away. The cottony seed heads had many traditional uses, including wound dressings, pillow stuffing, baby diapers, and wicks in oil lamps.

NODDING SEDGE
Carex gynandra
Sedge family (Cyperaceae)

Quick ID: Alternate leaves up to 5 per stem with bases wrapped in rough, brownish-red fibrous sheath; rough, 3-sided stems; separate staminate (male) and pistillate (female) flower spikes that droop with maturity: 2- to 5-inch pistillate spikes; 1- to 3-inch slender, pointed staminate spikes

Height: 18–60 inches

Sedges can be challenging to separate, as many look similar; but the nodding flower spikes of nodding sedge help identify this species. These can be found growing in moist areas, including swampy and boggy habitats. The roots, leaves, and stems of many *Carex* species were used in basketmaking.

NORTHERN LADY FERN

Athyrium angustum
Lady Fern family (Athyriaceae)
Quick ID: Bright green with lacy leaf blade, widest near middle

Height: 16–36 inches

A fern of the northeastern woods, northern lady fern has relatively large lacy fronds arising in a circle from a clump above the underground rhizome. To reflect recent genetic studies, a species change has moved this fern from *filix-femina* to *angustum*. In addition, this fern is now placed in the Lady Fern family (Athyriaceae) rather than Woodsiaceae; older field guides may not reflect these changes.

BRACKEN FERN
Pteridium aquilinum
Bracken Fern family (Dennstaedtiaceae)
Quick ID: Large, long arching stem; leaves at end
divided into 3 triangular parts

Height: 2–6 feet

Known worldwide, bracken fern can be found on
every continent except Antarctica. Ancient fern
fronds have been found in the fossil record from
over 55 million years ago. This fern does not grow
in clusters as many ferns do but is on individual
upright stems and forms large colonies. Although
the young fronds have been traditionally eaten
in spring and were made into a beer, it is now
known that bracken fern can cause stomach and
esophageal cancer and should not be ingested.
Growing in dry areas, bracken fern has a deep
rhizome that allows the plant to survive major
disturbances such as fire. The fronds were used
as thatch roofing and bedding for livestock, and
the rhizomes were used to make a yellow dye. The
rhizomes were also dried and used as a substitute
for flour in baking and as a treatment for worms.

HAYSCENTED FERN

Sitobolium punctilobulum

Bracken Fern family (Dennstaedtiaceae)

Quick ID: Deciduous; un-clustered single fronds covered with glandular hairs, yellowish green, lacy, narrow triangular

Height: 1–2 feet

Hayscented fern has fairly uniform-sized fronds and grows singly in colonies. Until recently, the scientific name of this fern was *Dennstaedtia punctilobula,* but genetic studies have demonstrated that it is more closely related to another species in Asia. If you gently rub the fronds of hayscented fern, they smell like fresh-mown hay. Hayscented fern has triangular fronds, unlike the fronds of New York fern, whose fronds taper to a point at the bottom.

MARGINAL WOOD FERN
Dryopteris marginalis
Shield Fern family (Dryopteridaceae)
Quick ID: evergreen; arching oblong cut into 15–29 pair of pinnae; leaflets longest toward middle of leaf; round sori (spore-bearing structures) at leaflet margins underneath

Height: 1–2 feet

The evergreen fronds of marginal wood fern, or marginal shield fern, can be found along damp, shady woodland trails. The spores of typical ferns are borne under the leaflets in dot-like structures called sori. A covering called an indusium may protect the sori. The marginal wood fern is named for its sori, which are found on the margin of each leaflet. Along with Christmas fern, marginal wood fern can survive the cold winters, and the evergreen fronds may be seen peeking through white blankets of snow.

EVERGREEN WOOD FERN
Dryopteris intermedia
Shield Fern family (Dryopteridaceae)

Quick ID: Evergreen; leaf blades arranged in circular cluster; leaf blades widest at base, tapering broadly toward the tip; compound leaves divided three times; leaf stalk scaly and hairy

Height: 18–36 inches

The large lacy fronds of evergreen wood fern form graceful arches in partial to full-shaded forests in the park. This fern has many common names, including fancy fern, glandular wood fern, intermediate shield fern, intermediate wood fern, and common wood fern. It is often confused with several other wood fern species, but if you look closely, the lowest leaflet closest to the stem is shorter than the next leaflet. In the spinulose wood fern (*D. carthusiana*), the lowest leaflet closest to the stem is longer than the next leaflet. Mountain wood fern (*D. campyloptera*) has the lowest leaflet closest to the stem and is much longer than the adjacent leaflet.

Sori of evergreen wood fern

Mountain wood fern

Spinulose wood fern

Close-up of spinulose wood fern

CHRISTMAS FERN
Polystichum acrostichoides
Wood Fern family (Dryopteridaceae)

Quick ID: Evergreen; fronds lance-shaped tapering leaflets eared at base; scales on leaf stalk

Height: 1–3 feet

One of the easiest ferns to identify, Christmas fern has shiny leathery fronds that grow in bouquet-like circular clusters from a central rootstock. The common name is derived from the leaflets, which are eared at the base, forming tiny boots that resemble Christmas stockings. Early settlers used the ferns as Christmas decorations.

NORTHERN OAK FERN
Gymnocarpium dryopteris
Brittle Fern family (Cystopteridaceae)
Quick ID: Small delicate, triangular fronds on single stems; deeply divided compound leaflets

Height: 6–18 inches

The northern oak fern, or oak fern, is found across North America and Eurasia. If you look under the triangular frond leaflets, or pinnae, you will find small round dots called sori, where the spores are found. Most ferns have a covering over the sori called an indusium, but northern oak fern lacks this covering, leading to the genus name, *Gymnocarpium*, which means "with naked fruit." The spores are adapted for wind dispersal. The plant produces new fronds all summer. Native Americans used the crushed leaves to repel mosquitoes. Look for this delicate fern growing in coniferous forests, on cliffs, and on rocky slopes. Surprisingly, oak ferns do not grow on or near oak trees. The common name oak fern is derived from the Greek words for oak (*drys*) and fern (*pteris*), which combine to form *dryopteris*.

SENSITIVE FERN
Onoclea sensibilis
Sensitive Fern family
(Onocleaceae)

Quick ID: Triangular leafy sterile fronds broadest near base, deeply lobed but not to stem (rachis); separate stalk with beaded dark spore cases

Height: 1–3 feet

One of the easiest ferns to identify, the broad, flat triangular fronds of sensitive ferns are unlike those of other common ferns found in Maine. Some people mistakenly think the fronds are sensitive to touch, but this fern is so named because the fronds wither at the first touch of frost. Lacking spores, the large triangular fronds are deeply lobed but not completely to the middle stem, called the rachis. The fertile fronds appear later as clusters of green beads that become brown. The beads are full of spores, leading to the alternate common name of bead fern. Sensitive ferns are common in wet areas such as bogs, marshes, and along stream banks. In the same family, the young curled tips, or "fiddleheads," of ostrich fern (*Matteuccia struthiopteris*) are gathered in parts of Maine and eaten as a spring vegetable. Although some ferns may be carcinogenic, ostrich ferns are considered safe to eat after 10 minutes of thorough cooking. Absent from the park, these delicious spring coils taste somewhat like asparagus, but it is extremely important to verify the species before eating.

Sori of sensitive fern

Ostrich fern

CINNAMON FERN
Osmundastrum cinnamomeum
Royal Fern family (Osmundaceae)

Quick ID: Arching circular clusters of fronds; frond broadest near middle, tapering to point at tip; tufts of reddish-brown hairs at base of leaflets; separate erect fertile spike with brownish spores

Height: 1–4 feet

Most ferns have their spores on the underside of their leaflets, but cinnamon fern is an exception to the rule, with long club-like fertile spikes producing the spores. From a distance, the fertile spikes resemble sticks of cinnamon, hence the common name. Forming large clumps from thick rhizomes, these ferns often form mounds on the ground in winter. Cinnamon fern is considered a "living fossil," as it has been found in the same form in the fossil record for 200 million years. The genus name is derived from Osmunder, the Saxon name for the god Thor. Cinnamon ferns thrive in wet shaded areas, often forming large waist-high colonies.

INTERRUPTED FERN
Claytosmunda claytoniana
Royal Fern family (Osmundaceae)
Quick ID: Leaves blunt ended, leaflets with rounded lobes; spores on fertile leaflets about one-third up stalk; lacks hairs at base of leaflets

Height: 2–4 feet

The interrupted fern is one of the most common ferns in Acadia. The broad fertile fronds of interrupted fern bear spores on small brown leaflets about one-third of the way up the stalk, "interrupting" the frond's flowing lines. These special leaflets are light brown when mature. The species name for interrupted fern, *claytoniana*, honors John Clayton (1686–1773), who made many important botanical discoveries in the New World. Interrupted ferns lack hairs at the base of the leaflets, distinguishing it from the similar cinnamon fern (*Osmundastrum cinnamomeum*).

Sori

Fronds interrupted by sori

ROYAL FERN
Osmunda regalis
Royal Fern family (Osmundaceae)
Quick ID: Clumps of large fronds; well separated leaflets (pinnae)

Height: 2–5 feet

A wetland species, royal fern is a very large fern that grows in clumps. The rootlike rhizomes often form large mounds from old leaf bases and are sometimes used by small mammals as shelter. The leaf bases have also been used as a medium in which to grow orchids. Found in bogs and marshes, the fertile spores are in brown clusters at the tips of the fronds.

ROCK POLYPODY
Polypodium virginianum
Polypody family (Polypodiaceae)
Quick ID: Evergreen; leathery fronds lobed and deeply cut, frond widest in middle; pinnae not divided
Height: 4–16 inches

Common rock polypody, or common rockcap fern, is a small evergreen fern that grows in mats on rocks. It needs only enough soil to get a foothold in tiny cracks on cliffs, often on north-facing rocks. On suitable habitat, it spreads by creeping rhizomes. Widespread in the East, rock polypody can be found from Greenland into Georgia. Native Americans used this fern for stomachaches, and it was made into a tea for heart disease.

NEW YORK FERN
Amauropelta noveboracensis
Marsh Fern family (Thelypteridaceae)
Quick ID: Yellow-green lacy fronds that taper at both ends; clumps of 3 or more fronds

Height: 8–25 inches

Found throughout the park in moist area, New York fern has distinctive fronds that taper at both ends. It grows in moist areas in clumps of three or more fronds. New York ferns prefer acidic soil and may become dominant in areas. New York fern has also been placed in other genera, including *Thelypteris* and *Parathelypteris*.

LONG BEECH FERN
Phegopteris connectilis
Marsh Fern family (Thelypteridaceae)
Quick ID: Narrow triangular fronds with tapered pointed tips; lowest leaflets (pinnae) pointing downward

Height: 6–14 inches

A hardy fern of the northlands, in the East long beech fern reaches its southernmost limits in Maryland and West Virginia, with disjunct populations in North Carolina and Tennessee. Also known as northern beech fern, narrow beech fern, or spearhead fern, this water-loving fern can be found along streams, in moist forests, or in the spray zone of waterfalls. Along with the downward-angled lower leaflets, the arching fronds taper at the tip and act as effective drip tips, allowing excess water to drip off the plant.

WOODLAND HORSETAIL
Equisetum sylvaticum
Horsetail family (Equisetaceae)

Quick ID: Round, hollow stem; distinct nodes surrounded by whorled horizontal drooping branches; terminal spore-bearing cone-like structure (strobilus)

Height: 10–27 inches

When you are looking at a horsetail, you may not realize that these are one of the most primitive plants, growing to the size of a tree during the Carboniferous period. The genus name, *Equisetum*, comes from the Latin *equis* ("horse") and *seta* ("bristle"), in reference to the resemblance to the tail of a horse. Found in wetland areas, woodland, or plumy, horsetail has lacy arching whorls of branches encircling the stem. Field horsetail (*E. arvense*) and water horsetail (*E. fluviatile*) are also found in the park but are not as delicately branched as woodland horsetail. Native Americans used the stems, which contain silica, to polish and scour objects.

COMMON CLUBMOSS
Lycopodium clavatum
Clubmoss family (Lycopodiaceae)
Quick ID: Creeping stems up to 10 feet long; upright branches average about 4 inches high with scalelike leaves; spores on tall branches (strobili)

Height: 2.0–5.9 inches

Known as fern allies, firmosses and clubmosses have more primitive characteristics than true ferns. Common clubmoss is also called staghorn clubmoss, running clubmoss, and ground pine, as it resembles tiny pine trees growing out of the ground. Millions of years ago, ancient clubmoss relatives reached 100 feet in height; we now use their fossilized remains as a source of power known as coal. The spores, borne on tall branches called strobili, are flammable and were once used as flash powder for photography. The spores were also used as a styptic and coagulant.

HAIRCAP MOSS
Polytrichum commune
Haircap Moss family (Polytrichaceae)
Quick ID: Wiry stalks with pointed lance-shaped leaves arranged in a spiral

Mosses do not have flowers or seeds. Periodically they produce thin stalks capped by spore capsules. When the capsules dry, they crack open and release spores that are scattered on the breeze to germinate new mosses. Along with mosses, liverworts and hornworts are two other groups of plants that typically lack vascular tissue and rely on absorption of water and nutrients through osmosis and diffusion. Found in most regions of the world, haircap moss is one of the most common of the about 15,000 species of moss in the world. Haircap mosses have been historically used for thousands of years as teas to dissolve gall bladder and kidney stones and to make brooms, brushes, baskets, and rugs.

PINCUSHION MOSS
Leucobryum glaucum
White Moss family (Leucobryaceae)
Quick ID: Dense rounded cushions or mats; light whitish green

Not all mosses grow on the north side of trees, as told in fables; most mosses grow on the dampest area of trees, regardless of the compass orientation. The pincushion moss is also called white cushion moss, as it forms rounded mounds of moss on the ground. *Leucobryum* means "white moss," as the leaves have a whitish cast that may help reflect light and allow this moss to live in drier areas than the moist habitats most mosses require. Due to their highly absorbent properties, mosses were traditionally used as diapers and for feminine hygiene.

PRAIRIE PEATMOSS
Sphagnum palustre
Sphagnum family (Sphagnaceae)
Quick ID: Narrow stem with smaller wavy branches from the main stem

Growing in wet forests and boggy areas, sphagnum moss is sometimes known as peat moss. The term "sphagnum moss" includes about 380 species, about 18 of which can be found in Acadia. Sphagnum can soak up water up to thirty times its own weight. The spores are distributed by shooting them under high velocity, using compressed air in the spore capsule. Due to its absorptive and antiseptic properties sphagnum has long been used as a dressing for wounds. It was also used as soap and skin care. Prairie peatmoss has green leaves, while with its distinctive red leaves, red peat moss (*S. rubellum*) creates distinctive carpets of rusty-wine color in cool habitats of North America.

Red peat moss

BOREAL LEAFY LIVERWORT
Bazzania trilobata
Lepidozia family (Lepidoziaceae)
Quick ID: Grows in clumps or mats on moist ground or logs; upper leaves overlapping lower leaves in 3 rows

Leafy liverworts look like mosses and have a similar life cycle, but if you look closely at the leaflets, they are typically in two ranks, with a smaller third row on the back of the stem rather than the spiral leaflet arrangement of mosses. Boreal leafy liverwort is also called greater whipwort. You can see this liverwort in mats on the forest floor on the Schoodic Peninsula. Scaleworts are leafy liverworts that look like the limbs of a tree branch pasted to a deciduous tree trunk such as red maple or beech. First collected in New York, the New York scalewort (*Frullania eboracensis*) is found in the eastern United States and north into Canada.

New York scalewort

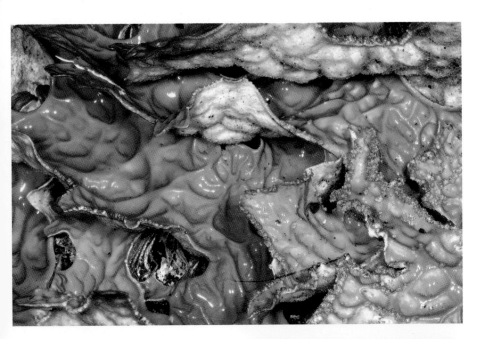

TREE LUNGWORT
Lobaria pulmonaria
Lungwort family (Lobariaceae)
Quick ID: Bright green when moist to brownish when dry; leafy with ridges

Type: Foliose (leafy)

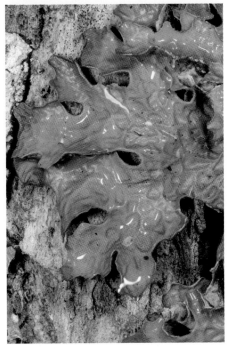

Lungwort has leafy green leathery lobes with veinlike ridges. Resembling thick lettuce leaves, these lobes are the body of the lichen, called the thallus. It is commonly seen growing on the bark of trees such as red maple. In the early 1600s it was widely believed that the character of a plant would determine its use. According to this "Doctrine of Signatures," lungwort, with ridges and pits that resemble lungs, could be used to treat respiratory problems. Lungworts have also been used to make dyes, perfumes, and even beer. Sensitive to air pollution, lungworts are able to survive only in areas where the air is clean.

MAP LICHEN
Rhizocarpon geographicum
Map Lichen family (Rhizocarpaceae)
Quick ID: Yellow tiles; black central dot

Type: Crustose (flat)

Pieced together like a stone walkway, the yellow map lichen grows very slowly. At a growth rate of about 0.44 inch per century, map lichens are used to determine the age of geologic events such as glacial retreat. In the Arctic, the map lichen has been aged at 8,600 years old, making it one of the world's oldest living organisms.

COMMON SUNBURST LICHEN
Xanthoria parietina
Sunburst Lichen family
(Teloschistaceae)

Quick ID: Flattened lobes; upper surface shades of orange, yellow, or greenish yellow; lower surface white

Type: Fruticose (shrubby)

Colorful sunburst lichens can be found in Acadia growing on rocks and tree branches. It contains a pigment called parietin, which gives this lichen its bright orange coloration. Normally growing on tree branches, it can also grow on rocks that are frequented by birds and other animals, which aid in the nutrient enrichment from their nitrogen-rich droppings. This lichen is spread in the fecal pellets of tiny mites that are commonly found in association with the lichen. Extracts of common sunburst lichen have been shown to inhibit viral replication. Following the "Doctrine of Signatures," historically it was used medicinally to treat jaundice due to its yellow color.

PINK EARTH LICHEN
Dibaeis baeomyces
Water and Whiteworm Lichen family (Icmadophilaceae)
Quick ID: Rounded pink heads; 0.04- to 0.24-inch pink stalk; chalky, grayish-white thallus

Type: Fruticose (shrubby)

Pink is an unusual color in nature, but the tiny pink fruiting bodies of pink earth lichen are eye-catching. The body of the lichen, called the thallus, hugs the bare ground and is grayish white and warty in appearance. It gives rise to the delicate pink reproductive structures that resemble tiny pink-topped candy pops. Hikers in the park should be careful where they place their feet to avoid damaging these and the more than 400 species of lichens found in Acadia.

FOAM LICHEN
Stereocaulon sp.
Snow Lichen family (Stereocaulaceae)
Quick ID: Grayish-white granular body (thallus)

Type: Fruticose (shrubby)

Found in the northeastern United States and Canada, ten species of foam lichens have been identified in Acadia. The spores are spread by wind and water, as well as by various animals. Foam lichens grow best at cool temperatures in the Northeast and at higher elevations further south, making these and other lichens susceptible to climate change. Lichens have an extremely slow growth rate, with some growing less than a millimeter per year. These fragile lichens grow on rocks and are easily damaged by trampling, so please share in the park's efforts to preserve these and other organisms.

BRITISH SOLDIER LICHEN
Cladonia cristatella
Spindles and Structured Lichen family
(Cladoniaceae)
Quick ID: Greenish-gray stalk; bright red caps

Type: Fruticose (shrubby)

In the world of lichens, perhaps none is so suitably named as the British soldier lichen. The red fruiting structure that sits atop a small greenish-gray stalk is named for the uniforms worn by British soldiers during the Revolutionary War. The main body of a lichen is called the thallus. The red tops are spore-producing bodies called apothecia. Lichens are typically named for their fungal part, in this case *Cladonia cristatella*; the algal part is *Trebouxia erici*. Through photosynthesis, the chlorophyll-containing alga provides energy and the fungal part provides water and nutrients in this mutualistic association. Lichens in this family have been used to produce a pinkish-red dye used to color cloth. Other lichens in this family include gritty soldier lichen (*C. floerkeana*), toy soldier lichen (*C. bellidiflora*), and pebbled pixie cup (*C. pyxidata*).

Gritty soldier lichen

Toy soldier lichen

Pebbled pixie cup

GRAY REINDEER LICHEN
Cladonia rangiferina
Spindles and Structured Lichen
family (Cladoniaceae)
Quick ID: Whitish to silvery gray;
cushion mounds

Type: Fruticose (shrubby)

In many areas of the park, you
may notice mats of silvery mounds
growing a few inches high on thin
soil. If you look closely at this lichen,
you will see small stems with
branches that look like tiny deer
antlers, hence the common name
reindeer lichen. Of course reindeer
are not found in Acadia National Park,
but in the far north this lichen is an
important food source for reindeer
(caribou). Many species of lichens
have unique biological properties that
allow their survival in challenging
ecological niches. Many lichens
are being studied for their medical
uses. Three lichens found in Acadia,
including gray reindeer lichen, have
been shown to degrade the deadly

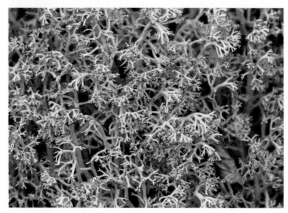

Close-up of gray reindeer lichen

Star-tipped reindeer lichen

prion protein that causes neurodegenerative diseases such as chronic wasting disease (CWD) and human
Creutzfeldt-Jakob disease (CJD). A similar lichen, star-tipped reindeer lichen (*C. stellaris*) forms on bare soil
or gravelly areas. According to the Canadian Museum of Nature, it has been named the unofficial national
lichen of Canada.

GIANT CLADONIA LICHEN
Cladonia maxima
Spindles and Structured Lichen family
(Cladoniaceae)
Quick ID: To 6 inches tall; light green to tan spindle like stems, some topped with pinkish caps

Type: Fruticose (shrubby)

Members of the genus *Cladonia* are sometimes called pixie cup lichens due to the cuplike caps atop their spindly, golf tee–like "stems." Giant cladonia lichens look like thick toothpicks stuck in the ground, some topped with a cuplike cap. A similar species, bighorn lichen (*C. cornuta*) looks like toothpicks with the top half coated in powdered sugar.

Close-up of giant cladonia lichen

Bighorn lichen

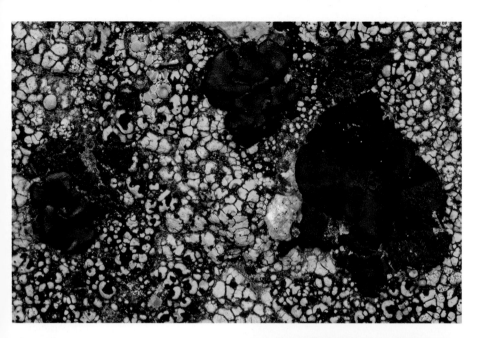

PEPPERED ROCK TRIPE
Umbilicaria deusta
Rock Tripe family (Umbilicariaceae)
Quick ID: Dark brown to black clusters, 0.4–2 inches in diameter; upper surface covered with tiny black granular dots; lower surface either smooth or covered with dimples

Type: Foliose (leaflike)

Rock tripes, or naval lichens, grow from a central "stalk" that is attached to the surface of a rock. The frayed edges are brittle when dry, but rock tripe becomes leathery when wet. Even though it apparently tastes like shoe leather, rock tripe has been used as a survival food; Native Americans added it to soups as a thickening agent. You can see this and many other lichens growing on the granite rocks in Acadia, including smooth rock tripe (*U. mammulata*) and common toadskin lichen (*Lasallia papulosa*).

Smooth rock tripe

Common toadskin lichen

231

BUSHY BEARD LICHEN
Usnea strigosa
Shield Lichen family (Parmeliaceae)
Quick ID: Long pale yellowish to grayish-green bristly strands; tips with yellowish hairy cups

Type: Fruticose (shrubby)

Lichens have three main forms, according to their shape. Crustose lichens are flat, foliose lichens are leafy, and fruticose lichens such as the bushy beard lichen are shrubby in appearance. Commonly known as "old man's beard," it hangs from trees like light grayish-green beards. Beard lichens contain a wide array of chemicals to fend off predators, including bacteria that would destroy them. These antibacterial properties are being studied as sources of medicines and for other valuable uses. The usnic acid in beard lichens has traditionally been used to treat wounds to prevent infection. This useful lichen was also used to make deodorants and dyes and to start fires. Some beard lichens look like fishbones hanging from the tree.

Old man's beard lichen

BOTTLEBRUSH SHIELD LICHEN
Parmelia squarrosa
Shield Lichen family
(Parmeliaceae)
Quick ID: Pitted greenish to white branches

Type: Foliose (leafy)

With lichens found worldwide, researchers are still finding new species. Growing on tree bark, bottlebrush shield lichen was described by Mason Hale, a Smithsonian leader in the study of mycology and lichenology. He recognized and collected the first

Common greenshield lichen

specimen in Shenandoah National Park in Virginia at 3,000 feet elevation. He noticed that the rootlike structures, called rhizinas, were relatively perpendicular. This species has also been discovered in eastern Asia, Nepal, Austria, and Switzerland. Another lichen in the same family, common greenshield lichen (*Flavoparmelia caperata*) also grows on trees and has wrinkled, rounded lobes.

CONCENTRIC RING LICHEN
Arctoparmelia centrifuga
Shield Lichen family (Parmeliaceae)
Quick ID: Yellowish-green body (thallus) with narrow lobes; lower surface felt-like white, brownish, or blackish

Type: Foliose (leafy)

Concentric ring lichen grows outward from the center then dies in the middle, creating a ring shape. The process often starts over again when a new patch forms in the center of the ring, creating a bull's-eye appearance. Like concentric ring lichen, Cumberland rock shield (*Xanthoparmelia cumberlandia*) also grows on rocks but doesn't grow in rings.

Cumberland rock shield

Close-up of Cumberland rock shield

GREEN STAIN FUNGUS
Chlorociboria aeruginascens
Cup Fungi family (Chlorociboriaceae)
Quick ID: Blue-green cup fungus with tiny cuplike fruiting bodies; green-stained wood

Green stain, or green wood cup, fungus is a saprotrophic mushroom that helps in the decay of fallen wood. Also known as green elfcup, the tiny, stalked cup-shaped fruiting bodies are not often seen. The green mycelium is prevalent on the rotting wood of oaks, poplar, and ash and contains a pigment called xylindein that stains the wood. Prized by woodworking artisans, the bluish-green stained wood was known as "green oak" and was used in the fifteenth century to add color to decorative wooden panels.

SWAMP BEACON
Mitrula elegans
Earth Tongue family (Sclerotiniaceae)
Quick ID: Bright yellow rounded to oblong cap on clear stem; grows in wetlands

With the appearance of small upright matchsticks, swamp, or bog, beacon looks like it might be a slime mold but is actually tiny fungi. The bright yellow caps stand out against the dark mucky areas in which they grow.

CROSS-VEINED TROOP MUSHROOM

Xeromphalina kauffmanii

Mycena family (Mycenaceae)

Quick ID: Clusters of small rusty-orange to cinnamon mushrooms; cap convex; creamy gills; brownish-red stem (stipe)

This tiny mushroom grows in large clusters on decaying logs of deciduous trees. It is commonly known as the cross-veined troop mushroom, as the gills are often connected by many crossveins. A mushroom of eastern forests, it has also been found in Costa Rica and Japan. Another nearly identical species, golden trumpet (*X. campanella*) grows on conifers. It is not considered edible; caution should be exercised, as many small brown mushrooms can be deadly if ingested. The species name honors American botanist and mycologist Calvin Henry Kauffman, who worked with the University of Michigan until the 1930s.

DESTROYING ANGEL
Amanita bisporigera
Amanita family (Amanitaceae)

Quick ID: Smooth white cap; white gills; white stalk with membranous white ring (annulus); white "sac" around base (volva)

Only a few poisonous mushrooms are actually fatal if eaten, but many of the deadly mushrooms look very similar to edible wild mushrooms. A beauty among its peers, this brilliant white mushroom radiates on the forest floor with a lovely lacy stalk skirt called an annulus and a white sac around the base called a volva. Very similar in appearance to edible meadow mushrooms and button mushrooms, the destroying angel, or death angel, has earned its name with fatal consequences. Considered to be the most toxic mushroom in North America, the destroying angel contains a highly poisonous toxin called amanitin that attacks the liver, central nervous system, and kidneys, killing the unfortunate victim within a week unless a liver transplant can be performed. Do not consume any mushroom unless you are absolutely sure of its identification.

YELLOW PATCHES
Amanita flavoconia
Amanita family (Amanitaceae)

Quick ID: Convex to flattened yellowish-orange cap with yellow warty patches; white gills; stalk pale yellow with yellow ring (annulus) and bulbous base with powdery yellow remnants of the volva

A beautiful mushroom, yellow patches is an Amanita with a yellowish-orange cap and pale yellow stem. It often has yellow patches on the cap that are remnants of the universal veil that covered the immature mushroom. This is one of the most common species of *Amanita* in eastern North America and the Midwest. Many *Amanita* species are poisonous, including yellow patches. It is mycorrhizal with oaks and other hardwoods and conifers but especially associated with hemlocks.

AMERICAN YELLOW FLY AGARIC
Amanita muscaria var. guessowii
Amanita family (Amanitaceae)
Quick ID: Yellow-orange cap with buffy white dots; creamy white gills; scurfy whitish stalk with ring (annulus) on upper stem and concentric scaly rings at base

With a colorful yellowish cap and white warty dots, the fly agaric is one of the most well-known mushrooms in the world. This mushroom has a number of color variations. The red-capped "toadstool" of *Alice in Wonderland* fame is more commonly found in western states. The common name, fly agaric, comes from the use of bits of the mushroom placed in a bowl of milk to attract and kill flies. The mushroom is poisonous and hallucinogenic, as it contains two toxins, ibotenic acid and muscimol.

RED RUSSULA
Russula sp.
Russula family (Russulaceae)
Quick ID: Cap red (variable); white gills; white stem

Russulas are a widespread group of more than 750 mushrooms that often have red caps, but they also can range from yellow to green. They are often called brittlegills because when flicked with your finger, the gills often flake off like brittle sliced almond–like chips. Like many species of mushrooms, russulas are mycorrhizal, meaning they live in a symbiotic relationship with a tree or other plant. The fungus gets nourishment from the tree in the form of sugars and the tree gains water from the fungus as well as essential nutrients. The North American Mycological Association (namyco.org) and local clubs sponsor mushroom forays to determine the variety of species of fungi and to encourage much-needed research in the field of mycology.

BLACK TRUMPET
Craterellus fallax
Chanterelle family (Cantharellaceae)
Quick ID: Vase shaped, 1–3.5 inches tall; grayish black upper surface; false gills on the stem (stipe)

In mid- to late summer after a cooling rain, mushrooms begin to pop up under the moist forest canopy. Some mushrooms are colorful, adding to the beauty of the forests, but one mushroom is grayish black and quite challenging to see among the leaf litter. You may smell the earthy, fruity odor of the funnel-shaped black trumpet mushroom before you see it. It grows under deciduous trees such as oaks, beeches, and maples. Also known as horn of plenty, trumpet of the dead, and devil's horn, the imaginative common names refer to the impression that the funnel-shaped black trumpets are being played from under the ground. In the same family as black trumpets, many other species of chanterelles can be found here, including golden chanterelle (*C. cibarius*), yellowfoot chanterelle (*C. tubaeformis*), and red chanterelle (*C. cinnabarinus*). To maintain the biodiversity of the park, it is against the law to pick mushrooms in Acadia.

POPLAR OYSTER MUSHROOM

Pleurotus populinus

Pleurotus family (Pleurotaceae)

Quick ID: Fan-shaped grayish-white cap up to 9 inches wide; grayish-white gills running down the stalk; stalk short or lacking, bunched together on wood of poplars

With their characteristic oyster shape, oyster mushrooms are a choice edible with a light taste and may be found in many grocery stores. Genetic research has shown that there are several species of oyster mushrooms, including the poplar oyster mushroom. As its common name implies, it grows on poplars in the Northeast. Long used in folk medicine, the health benefits of mushrooms such as the oyster mushroom are in further need of study. Highly nutritious oyster mushrooms are high in selenium, potassium, and B vitamins; oyster mushrooms are also high in antioxidants that fight free radicals and may help lower the risk of cancer. They also may reduce cholesterol, improve cognitive health, and control blood sugar levels.

UPRIGHT CORAL MUSHROOM
Ramaria stricta
Gomphoid family (Gomphaceae)
Quick ID: Clump of multiple slender, parallel, upright branches; yellowish fading to buffy

The upright coral mushroom grows in forested areas in Acadia. Resembling ocean corals, it grows in branching 3.5-inch clumps on dead wood that is often buried beneath the surface of the soil. Several varieties have been described, some of which can only be distinguished by microscopic characteristics. It is not considered edible, as it has a bitter taste and unpleasant odor. Other types of coral fungi may have more or less branching or none at all and come in a variety of colors, including orange, white, yellow, and red.

RED-MOUTH BOLETE
Boletus subvelutipes
Bolete family (Boletaceae)
Quick ID: Cap various shades of red, brown, yellow; red pores stain blue; stalk red, brown, and orange, often with hairs at base

Like many mushrooms, the red-mouth bolete has a mycorrhizal association with oaks and pines such as hemlock in which both organisms benefit from the association. These mushrooms have been used to make light brown dyes for wool and fabrics. If you gently lift up the cap to peek under it, your finger may leave a blue spot on the underside pores. Another bolete, the bay bolete (*Imleria badia*, or *Boletus badius*) has a flattened reddish-brown cap. The yellow pores stain light bluish green when pressed. Some boletes such as bay boletes are edible, but red-mouth boletes are poisonous. Never eat any wild mushrooms without an expert identification. In Acadia National Park, it is not permitted to pick any mushrooms at all, so foragers will have to seek their specimens elsewhere.

Bay bolete

Bay bolete pores

BIRCH POLYPORE
Fomitopsis betulina
Bracket Polypore family (Fomitopsidaceae)
Quick ID: Polypore; tan to brown with thick, rolled-over margin; white pores that turn brown; stubby stem

Birch polypore is a type of saprophytic bracket fungus that only grows on birch trees. It is rounded to hoof shaped with white to brownish pores underneath. The leatherlike surface was used to sharpen razors, earning it the name "razor strop" fungus. Birch polypores have long been used for their medicinal properties. Two pieces of the mushroom were found with the 5,300-year-old mummified Iceman found in a glacier in the Italian Alps. The mushroom has antimicrobial, antiviral, and anti-inflammatory properties and potential anticancer properties. Perhaps the Iceman relied on this polypore for the medicinal properties attributed to this unassuming mushroom.

NORTHERN RED BELTED CONK

Fomitopsis mounceae
Bracket Polypore family (Fomitopsidaceae)
Quick ID: Polypore; fan-shaped; brown or red bands, bumpy warty when aged; sticky, resinous coating; underside yellowish white

The northern red belted conk is a woody shelf fungus that grows on dead or dying poplars or coniferous trees. As the result of genetic analyses, in 2019 mycologists determined that the red belted conk was three different species. The eastern species was long thought to be *F. pinicola*, but that species is actually found only in Europe and Asia. The third species, *F. schrenkii*, is found only at high elevations in the Rocky Mountains. Our species in the East, *F. mounceae*, was named for Irene Mounce, a Canadian mycologist.

RUBUS ORANGE RUST
Gymnoconia peckiana
Rust Fungus family (Phragmidiaceae)
Quick ID: Masses of bright orange spots (spores) on underside of blackberry leaves

Orange rust is a fungal disease of blackberries in the Northeast. There are approximately 7,000 species of rusts, which are fungi that cause diseases in a variety of plants. One such rust infects blackberries and raspberries, covering the lower surface of the leaves with masses of orange spores that affect the health of the plant. The orange spores are spread by the wind to infect other plants. The fungus infects the entire plant and survives the winter in the roots and stems.

WOLF'S MILK SLIME
Lycogala epidendrum
Plasmodial Slime Mold family (Tubiferaceae)
Quick ID: Small round spheres; variable color from pink to black; grows on wood

Found on rotting wood, slime molds were originally placed in the kingdom Fungi, but recent studies have shown that of slime molds are not related to true fungi; they are now placed in the phylum Amoebozoa, along with amoeboid protozoans. Wolf's milk slime mold oozes a red gel if damaged. Resembling spilled scrambled eggs, the "dog vomit" slime mold (*Fuligo septica*) is a brilliant yellow moving blob that often grows in mulch.

Dog vomit slime mold

WILLOW PINECONE GALL
Rabdophaga strobiloides
Gall Midge family (Cecidomyiidae)
Quick ID: Gray to brown pinecone-like structure on willow stems

If you see what appears to be a pinecone growing on a willow, you are looking at the willow pinecone gall. It is caused by a midge insect that lays its eggs on the stems of willows; in response, the willow forms a gall out of its own plant tissues around the eggs.

CHERRY FINGER GALL
Eriophyes cerasicrumena
Gall and Rust Mite family (Eriophyidae)
Quick ID: Small pouch-like green structures that turn into red fingers on the upper side of cherry leaves

Numerous small red fingerlike projections on the upper side of the leaves of cherry are caused by a tiny eriophyid mite. The galls are the larval food for the cherry gall azure butterfly, a recently described species that should be looked for in June in Acadia. Different species of azures fly in different time periods.

SPRUCE PINEAPPLE GALL ADELGID
Adelges abietis
Adelgid family (Adelgidae)
Quick ID: Small brown pineapple-shaped gall on the twigs of spruce

Resembling tiny pinecones on the twigs of spruce, the pineapple-shaped galls are often confused with the actual cones of the tree. Introduced from Europe, the pineapple gall adelgid is a tiny insect that is related to aphids. When the insect lays its eggs on the twig of a conifer tree, it causes the plant to form a pineapple-shaped outgrowth of plant tissue.

GOLDENROD GALL FLY
Eurosta solidaginis
Peacock Fruit Fly family (Tephritidae)
Quick ID: Round to oval, 1 inch long, greenish with some parts wine red in color about three-quarters of the way up the stem

You may notice unusual greenish rounded bumps on the stem of large goldenrods, especially tall goldenrod (*Solidago altissima*). They are galls caused by a small fruit fly that lays up to one hundred eggs in the terminal bud using a tubelike structure called an ovipositor. After about a week, the eggs hatch and the larvae chew through the bud into the stem. The saliva of the larva stimulates the plant to form a gall from its own tissues . In fall, the gall dries into a hard protective case around the larva, which emerges the next spring. Birds such as woodpeckers, chickadees, and wild turkeys learn there is a tasty snack inside the gall.

ALDER TONGUE FUNGUS
Taphrina robinsoniana
Leaf Curl Fungus family (Taphrinaceae)
Quick ID: Fleshy reddish to blackish tonguelike projections from cones of alders

Commonly seen on the cones of alders, the alder tongue fungus causes 1-inch-long fleshy tonguelike structures that turn hard and black with age. These strange projections are caused by a yeast-like fungus that is carried by the wind.

BIRCH BLISTER APHID GALL
Hamamelistes betulinus
Aphid family (Aphididae)
Quick ID: Large green blisters on birch leaves

A conspicuous gall caused by an aphid, which causes the plant to produce enlarged blister-like growths on the leaves of birch.

CADILLAC MOUNTAIN GRANITE

Quick ID: Flecks of pink and black minerals

Type: Igneous rock

Granite is a white or grayish igneous rock with grains of various colors. Igneous rocks are formed from magma deep below the Earth's surface. Formed about 420 million years ago, Cadillac Mountain Granite has a characteristic pink coloration from the high amount of potassium feldspar. It is blended with black hornblende and white quartz. There are other types of granite here, but Cadillac Mountain Granite is the most prominent. After the granite formed under great pressure, it took millions of years for water, wind, and waves to erode the surface down to the granite floor we see today.

ELLSWORTH SCHIST

Quick ID: Dark green to gray, streaked appearance; lighter-colored layers of quartz and feldspar mixed with the darker mineral chlorite

Type: Metamorphic rock

Schist is a type of metamorphic rock that is layered and tends to break along the layering. Schist is similar to the more familiar slate that also breaks along layers, but schist splits in more-irregular patterns. Ellsworth Schist is the oldest exposed rock on Mount Desert Island. You can find large outcrops at the Thompson Island Picnic Area.

REFERENCES

Arora, D. *Mushrooms Demystified.* 2nd ed. Berkeley, CA: Ten Speed Press, 1986.

Arsenault, M., et al. *Sedges of Maine: A Field Guide to Cyperaceae.* Orono: The University of Maine Press, 2013.

Braun, D., and R. Braun. *Guide to the Geology of Mount Desert Island and Acadia National Park.* Berkeley, CA: North Atlantic Books, 2016.

Brinkley, E. S. *Field Guide to Birds of North America.* New York: Sterling Publishing Co., 2008.

Brodo, I. M., S. D. Sharnoff, and S. Sharnoff. *Lichens of North America.* New Haven, CT: Yale University Press, 2001.

Burk, J. S. *The Wildlife of New England: A Viewer's Guide.* Durham: University of New Hampshire Press, 2011.

Butcher, R. D. *Field Guide to Acadia National Park, Maine.* Lanham, MD: Taylor Trade Publishing, 2005.

Capinera, J. L., R. D. Scott, and T. J. Walker. *Field Guide to Grasshoppers, Katydids, and Crickets of the United States.* Ithaca, NY: Cornell University Press, 2004.

Cobb, B. *A Field Guide to Ferns and Their Related Families.* New York: Houghton Mifflin, 1984.

Conant, R., and J. T. Collins. *A Field Guide to Reptiles & Amphibians: Eastern and Central North America.* 3rd ed. New York: Houghton Mifflin Company, 1998.

Eckstorm, F. H. *Handicrafts of the Modern Indians of Maine.* Bar Harbor, ME: Abbe Museum, 2003.

Elliman, T., and New England Wild Flower Society. *Wildflowers of New England.* Portland, OR: Timber Press, 2016.

Glassberg, J. *Butterflies through Binoculars: The East.* New York: Oxford University Press, 1999.

Gosner, K. L. *Atlantic Seashore: Peterson Field Guides.* Boston: Houghton Mifflin Company, 1978.

Gracie, C. *Spring Wildflowers of the Northeast.* Princeton, NJ: Princeton University Press, 2012.

———. *Summer Wildflowers of the Northeast.* Princeton, NJ: Princeton University Press, 2020.

Grierson, R. G. *Wildlife Watcher's Guide: Acadia National Park.* Minocqua, WI: NorthWord Press, 1995.

Holland, M. *Naturally Curious*. North Pomfret, VT: Trafalgar Square Books, 2019.

Howell, S. N. G., and B. L. Sullivan. *Offshore Sea Life ID Guide: East Coast*. Princeton, NJ: Princeton University Press, 2016.

Johnson, B. *The Heritage of Our Maine Wildflowers*. Rockland, ME: Courier of Maine Books, 1978.

Kaczmarek, F. *New England Wildflowers*. Guilford, CT: FalconGuides, Morris Book Publishing, LLC, 2009.

Kaiser, J. *Acadia: The Complete Guide*. 5th ed. Chicago: Independent Publishers Group, Destination Press, 2018.

Kaufman, K., and K. Kaufman. *Kaufman Field Guide to Nature of New England*. Boston: Houghton Mifflin Harcourt, 2012.

Kong, D., and D. Ring. *Best Easy Day Hikes Acadia National Park*. Guilford, CT: Falcon-Guides, 2015.

Lovitch. D., ed. *Birdwatching in Maine*. Hanover, NH: University Press of New England, 2017.

Marchand, P. J. *Nature Guide to the Northern Forest: Exploring the Ecology of the Forests of New York, New Hampshire, Vermont, and Maine*. Boston: Appalachian Mountain Club Books, 2010.

McBride, B., and H. E. L. Prins. *Indians in Eden: Wabanakis & Rusticators on Maine's Mount Desert Island 1840–1920*. Camden, ME: Down East Books, 2009.

Miller, D. S. *The Maine Coast: A Nature Lover's Guide*. Charlotte, NC: Fast & McMillan Publishers, East Woods Press, 1979.

Milne, L., and M. Milne, *The Audubon Society Field Guide to North American Insects and Spiders*. New York: Chanticleer Press, Inc., 1980.

Minetor, R., and N. Minetor. *Best Easy Bird Guide Acadia National Park*. Guilford, CT: FalconGuides, 2021.

———. *Birding New England*. Guilford, CT: FalconGuides, 2019.

Mittelhauser, G. H., et al. *The Plants of Acadia National Park*. Orono: The University of Maine Press, 2010.

Neves, L. *Northeast Medicinal Plants*. Portland, OR: Timber Press, Inc., 2020.

Newlin, W. V. P. *Lakes & Ponds of Mt. Desert*. Berkeley, CA: North Atlantic Books, 2013.

Opler, P. A., and V. Malikul. *A Field Guide to Eastern Butterflies*. New York: Houghton Mifflin Harcourt, 1992.

Page, L .M., and B. M. Burr. *Peterson Field Guide to Freshwater Fishes of North America North of Mexico*. 2nd ed. New York: Houghton Mifflin Harcourt, 2011.

Petrides, G. A. *A Field Guide to Trees and Shrubs.* 2nd ed. New York: Houghton Mifflin Co., 1986.

Reid, F. A. *Peterson Field Guides: Mammals of North America.* 4th ed. Boston: Houghton Mifflin Co., 2006.

Sept, J. D. *Atlantic Seashore Field Guide: Florida to Canada.* Mechanicsburg, PA: Stackpole Books, 2016.

Shumway, S. W. *Atlantic Seashore: Beach Ecology from the Gulf of Maine to Cape Hatteras.* Guilford, CT: FalconGuides, 2008.

Sibley, D. A. *National Audubon Society: The Sibley Guide to Birds.* 2nd ed. New York: Alfred A. Knopf, 2014.

Steele, F. L. *At Timberline: A Nature Guide to the Mountains of the Northeast.* Boston: Appalachian Mountain Club, 1982.

Helpful Websites

Animal Diversity Web: animaldiversity.org

Cornell Lab of Ornithology: allaboutbirds.org

Cornell Lab of Ornithology—Merlin Bird ID: merlin.allaboutbirds.org

Go Botany: gobotany.nativeplanttrust.org

Hawk Migration Association of North America: hmana.org

iNaturalist: inaturalist.org

GLOSSARY

achene: dry, one-seeded fruits with the outer wall enclosing the seed

alkaloid: bitter compounds produced by plants to discourage predators

alternate leaves: growing singly on a stem without an opposite leaf

anadromous: fish migration from ocean to fresh waters to spawn

anther: tip of a flower's stamen that produces pollen grains

arboreal: living in trees

basal: at the base

Batesian mimicry: a form of deception where a harmless species imitates the appearance of a dangerous one to avoid predators

blade: leaf or other flat, broad portion of a plant

bulb: underground structure made up of layered, fleshy scales

cache: food storage area

capsule: a dry fruit that releases seeds through splits or holes

carapace: upper (dorsal) shell of a turtle, crustacean, or arachnid

carrion: remains of deceased animal

catkin: a spike, either upright or drooping, of tiny flowers

commensalism: a type of symbiosis where one species benefits while a second species is neither harmed nor benefited

compound leaf: a leaf that is divided into two or more leaflets

corm: rounded, solid underground stem

deciduous: a tree that seasonally loses its leaves

disjunct: species that are geographically separated

diurnal: active by day

Downeast or Down East: a phrase that comes from sailing terminology. Sailors from ports in the west such as Boston sailed downwind toward the east to reach more-northern ports. Generally, the term refers to the northeast coastal section of Maine and the Canadian Maritime Provinces.

drupe: outer fleshy fruit usually having a single hard pit that encloses a seed

ecosystem: a biological environment consisting of all the living organisms in a particular area as well as nonliving components such as water, soil, air, and sunlight

endemic: growing only in a specific region or habitat

ethnobotany: the study of the relationship between plants and people

evergreen: a tree that keeps its leaves (often needles) year-round

exoskeleton: rigid external body covering, found especially in arthropods

frond: fern leaf, made up of the blade and stipe

genus: taxonomic rank below family and above species; always capitalized and italicized

glean: pick small insects from foliage

habitat: the area or environment where an organism lives or occurs

host: an organism that harbors another organism

intertidal: the area of shoreline between the highest and lowest reaches of the tide

introduced: a species living outside its native range; often introduced by human activity

leaflet: a part of a compound leaf; may resemble an entire leaf but it is borne on a vein of a leaf rather than the stem. Leaflets are referred to as pinnae; the compound leaves are pinnate (feather-like).

local resident: nonmigratory species found year-round in an area; also "resident"

marsupial: class of mammals that carry young in a pouch

metamorphic rock: a rock that has been altered by extreme heat and pressure, such as gneiss, schist, or quartzite

migration: movement of birds between breeding grounds and wintering areas

mutualism: a type of symbiosis where both organisms benefit

mycorrhiza (pl. mycorrhizae): the symbiotic mutually beneficial relationship between a fungus and the roots of a plant

nape: area at back of the head

native: a species indigenous or endemic to an area

nectar: sweet liquid produced by flowers to attract pollinators

niche: an organism's response to available resources and competitors (like a human's job)

nocturnal: active at night

omnivore: feeds on a variety of foods, including both plant and animal materials

opposite leaves: growing in pairs along the stem

parasitism: one organism benefiting at the expense of another organism

pollen: small powdery particles that contain the plant's male sex cells

pollination: transfer of pollen from an anther (male) to a stigma (female)

proboscis: a tubular mouthpart insects use for feeding and sucking

refugia: relict population

rhizome: underground stem that grows horizontally and sends up shoots

saprophyte: a plant, fungus, or microorganism that lives on dead or decaying organic matter

scute: thickened horny or bony plate, as on a turtle's shell

sepal: usually green leaflike structures found underneath the flower

species: taxonomic rank below genus; always italicized but never capitalized; also called "specific epithet"

spore: reproductive cell that can develop into a new individual asexually in organisms including fungi, ferns, and lichens

stamen: male part of the flower composed of a filament, or stalk, and anther, the sac at the tip of the filament that produces pollen

stipe: stalklike structure

symbiosis: association of unlike organisms that benefits one or both

taxonomy: study of scientific classifications

toothed: jagged or serrated edge

torpor: short-term state of decreased physiological activity, including reduced body temperature and metabolic rate

wing bar: line of contrastingly colored plumage formed by the tips of the flight feathers of birds

winged: thin, flattened expansion on the sides of a plant part

INDEX

ABOUT THE AUTHORS

As professional photographers, biologists, and authors, **Ann and Rob Simpson** are noted national park experts, having spent years involved with research and interpretation in US national parks. They have written numerous books on national parks from coast to coast that promote wise and proper use of natural habitats and environmental stewardship. In cooperation with American Park Network, both have led Canon "Photography in the Parks" workshops in major national parks, including Grand Canyon, Yellowstone, Yosemite, and Great Smoky Mountains.

Ann teaches biology at Laurel Ridge Community College in Middletown, Virginia. Rob is retired from teaching natural resources at the college. As a former chief of interpretation and national park board member, Rob has a unique understanding of the inner workings of the national park system. The Simpsons regularly lead international photo tours to parks and natural history destinations around the world. They are members of the following professional organizations: Outdoor Writers Association of America (OWAA), Virginia Outdoor Writers Association of America (VOWA), Mason-Dixon Outdoor Writers Association (M-DOWA), North American Nature Photography Association (NANPA), and Virginia Native Plant Society (VNPS).

Long known for their stunning images of the natural world, their work has been widely published in magazines such as *National Geographic, Time, National Wildlife*, and *Ranger Rick*, as well as many calendars, postcards, and books. You can see their work at Simpsons' Nature Photography (agpix.com/snphotos).